BISHOP FELL AND NONCONFORMITY

**OXFORDSHIRE
LIBRARY SERVICE**

3302806139	
ORS	8·1·2016
LS942.57 WITN	
0902509187	

The Oxfordshire Record Society

BISHOP FELL AND NONCONFORMITY:

VISITATION DOCUMENTS FROM THE OXFORD DIOCESE, 1682–83

Edited by Mary Clapinson

VOLUME LII

Issued for the years 1977 and 1978

1980

This Edition © Oxfordshire Record Society 1980

ISBN 0 902509 14 4

Printed in England by
W. S. MANEY AND SON LIMITED
HUDSON ROAD LEEDS

TABLE OF CONTENTS

		page
	FOREWORD	vii
	LIST OF ABBREVIATIONS	viii
	INTRODUCTION	xi
I	Letters to Fell from Oxfordshire Incumbents, 1682	1
II	Fell's Queries and his Archdeacon's Replies, 1682	33
III	The Archdeacon's List of Dissenters, 1683	37
	APPENDIX The Return of Conventicles in the Oxford Diocese, 1669	40
	NOTES	48
	INDEXES	75

FOREWORD

The letters printed in Part I of this volume were first transcribed by Mr Ian Philip, then Keeper of Printed Books in the Bodleian Library; Mr Philip most generously later placed his transcripts at the disposal of his colleague Mrs Clapinson, who has provided an Introduction, sought out further documents (three of them printed here in full), and carried out the onerous task of annotation of the complete text.

The Society is most grateful to the Governing Body of Christ Church, Oxford, for a substantial grant (from a benefaction made by the late Lt.Col. H. K. Sadler, D.S.O., M.C., sometime Commoner of the House) towards the publication of a volume concerned with the activities as Bishop of one of the most notable Deans of Christ Church.

Christ Church, Oxford J. F. A. MASON
February 1980 *Hon. Editor, O.R.S.*

LIST OF ABBREVIATIONS

Besse, *Sufferings*	Joseph Besse, *A Collection of the Sufferings of the People called Quakers* (London, 1753)
Bodl.	Bodleian Library, Oxford
Cal. S.P.Dom.	*Calendar of State Papers Domestic*
Calamy	Edmund Calamy, *An Account of the Ministers, Lecturers . . . who were ejected or silenced in 1660* (London, 1713)
Calamy Revised	A. G. Matthews, *Calamy Revised* (Oxford, 1934)
Catholic Missions	Mrs B. Stapleton, *A History of the Post-Reformation Catholic Missions in Oxfordshire* (London, 1900)
DNB	*Dictionary of National Biography*
Freedom after Ejection	Alexander Gordon, *Freedom after Ejection* (Manchester, 1917)
H.M.C.	Reports of the Historical Manuscripts Commission
Hassall	W. O. Hassall, 'Papists in early 18th century Oxfordshire', *Oxoniensia*, XIII (1948), 76–82
Lyon Turner	G. Lyon Turner, *Early Records of Nonconformity*, 3 vols (London, 1911–12)
MS. Archd. pprs. Oxon.	Oxford Archdeaconry Papers in the Bodleian Library
MS. Oxf. Dioc.	Oxford Diocesan Papers in the Bodleian Library
MS. Rawl.	Rawlinson manuscripts in the Bodleian Library
O.R.O.	Oxfordshire County Record Office
O.R.S.	Oxfordshire Record Society
Oldfield	Canon W. J. Oldfield, Calendar of the Records of Oxfordshire Quarter Sessions (typescript, in Oxfordshire County Record Office)

Oxon. Peculiars	S. A. Peyton, *The Churchwardens' presentments in the Oxfordshire Peculiars of Dorchester, Thame and Banbury*, Oxfordshire Record Society, x (1928)
Secker Visitation	H. A. Lloyd Jukes, *Articles of Enquiry Addressed to the Clergy of the Diocese of Oxford at the Primary Visitation of Dr. Thomas Secker, 1738*, Oxfordshire Record Society, xxxviii (1957)
V.C.H., Oxon.	*Victoria County History of Oxfordshire* (i, ed. L. F. Salzman; ii, ed. W. Page; iii, ed. H. E. Salter and Mary D. Lobel; iv and x, ed. A. Crossley; v–viii, ed. M. D. Lobel; ix, ed. M. D. Lobel and A. Crossley)

All manuscripts referred to are in the Bodleian Library, unless otherwise stated.

References to the number of nonconformists and papists in 1676 are from the Compton Census, see below, p. xix.

INTRODUCTION

When John Fell became Bishop of Oxford in 1676, he had already devoted fifteen years of his life, as Dean of Christ Church, to reforming and revitalizing that institution after the troubles of the 1640s and 1650s. At the beginning of the civil war, as a Student of Christ Church, Fell had taken up arms for the King, and had served in the Oxford garrison, with many other undergraduates, until its fall in June 1646. In 1648, Fell was, like most Royalists, ejected from his college post by order of the Parliamentary Visitors. Thirty-six years later, Fell described the effect on the university of the Parliamentary Visitation as he saw it:

within the compass of few weeks an almost general riddance was made of the loial University of Oxford; in whose room succeeded an illiterate rabble, swept up from the plough tail, from shops and grammar Scholes, and the dregs of the neighbor University.[1]

Fell had been ordained in 1647 and after his ejection continued to live in Oxford, one of a small group of clergy who celebrated in private the rites of the Anglican church for those who, like John Evelyn in London, always adhered to the form and usage of the Book of Common Prayer, despite its being declared illegal.[2] The portrait of Fell with John Dolben and Richard Allestree by Sir Peter Lely, now in Christ Church, commemorates this association. At the Restoration, he returned to Christ Church and, becoming Dean in November 1660, set about the task, as he saw it, of rescuing it from the decay of principles, the abolition of discipline and the growth of atheism and enthusiasm of the previous twelve years, with a zeal which must have alarmed more hesitant supporters of the new regime. Nathaniel Salmon gives a sketch of Fell's activities which is awe-inspiring in the energy it displays:

The Dean set himself as a bulwark against these corruptions, and as a faithful guardian to the youth of his College, and enquired into the behaviour of them all. He would see that they attended both the Chapel and the Hall; esteeming those Noblemen and Gentlemen Commoners, who would reckon themselves above discipline, to be but a splendid nuisance to the University, who, by their example and their purse, would influence the Scholars, he either reformed their manners

---

[1] In his preface to Richard Allestree, *Forty Sermons* (Oxford and London, 1684).
[2] *The Diary of John Evelyn*, ed. E. S. de Beer (Oxford, 1955), III, 90.

or sent them away . . . . He . . . would not suffer his College to be a place of no improvement like Bath or Newmarket, to pass away some idle time . . .³

He even made regular visits to the students' rooms and checked on the progress they were making in their studies. An interesting example of Fell's supervision of an individual student is given in letters to James, Duke of Ormonde, Chancellor of the University, while his grandson, James, was at Christ Church.⁴ Peter Drelincourt, servant to the Duke, reported several times on Fell's care of the boy. In July 1679 he wrote that the Dean frequently came unexpectedly to see Lord James, to discover what he was doing, to read a little with him, and to set him passages of classical authors to learn. At the end of August he wrote that the Dean continued 'extremely kind to and careful of his lordship'.⁵ Fell himself often wrote of the boy's progress to his grandfather.

As Vice-Chancellor from 1666 to 1669, Fell extended the same care to the whole of the university.⁶ He restored order and discipline to the disputations, lectures and examinations, frequently attending them in person to ensure that all duties were properly fulfilled. Salmon tells us that the improvements effected by Fell surprised all his friends — 'He exceeded their expectation by his firmness and application, standing in awe of none of those little considerations which divert and biass men of less diligence and zeal.'⁷ Throughout his life Fell was generous in providing money both for public concerns and for deserving scholars. His activities were not restricted to the disciplinary and pastoral aspects of the university. He did much to improve the University Press and its style of printing, providing it with matrices and punches of the best types available, putting the financing of the printing work on a surer footing, and arranging the publication of some classical author each year. He persuaded Archbishop Sheldon to give money for the building of a theatre, to serve as a more suitable place for university ceremonies than St Mary's church. Probably his most lasting monument in Oxford is in the buildings of his own

---

³ Nathaniel Salmon, *The Lives of the English Bishops from the Restauration to the Revolution* (London, 1733), 314.

⁴ *H.M.C.*, Ormonde, 36 (1908), passim.

⁵ *H.M.C.*, Ormonde, 36 (1908), 156, 195.

⁶ Anthony Wood noted that 'the Chancellor [Lord Clarendon] in his letters for Dr. Fell to be Vice Chancellor saith that Dr. Fell having shewne himself so able in governing the greatest college in the University, will be fit to be trusted with the government of the University itself, and will in this office apply himself with the same zeal he has shown in his private college, to the encouragement of learning and virtue and the suppressing vice and disorder'. *The Life and Times of Anthony Wood*, ed. Andrew Clark, II, 82–83 n. (O.H.S., XXI, 1892).

⁷ Nathaniel Salmon, *The Lives of the English Bishops*, p. 315.

college, and especially in the famous Tom Tower, which he engaged Christopher Wren to design and build in 1681–82.[8]

Fell's reputation as an energetic and dedicated Dean long survived him in his college. Dr William Stratford of Christ Church, in his letters to Edward, later Lord Harley, in the second and third decades of the eighteenth century, often referred to Fell, as one 'who . . . stretched the authority of the Dean to the utmost', who suppressed the riotous breakfast on 'Egg Saturday before Lent', and whose ghost was reckoned to be 'in great agonies of mind for his College' over the actions of a successor to Henry Aldrich in 1712.[9] As late as 1725, Stratford, commenting on the fact that the Dean, with the Bishops of Gloucester and Llandaff, had sat late over lunch in the deanery and not attended the sermon in the cathedral, speculated that Fell's ghost probably walked in protest at such indisciplined behaviour.[9]

There can be no doubt that Fell was a man of exemplary character in his private devotion and in the energy and zeal with which he served the public — both characteristics which must have marked him out as a suitable candidate for a bishopric. His loyalty to the monarchy and the Anglican church had always been his guiding principle. In 1659, when the failure of Richard Cromwell as Lord Protector became apparent and opened up the possibility of a new political settlement, Fell published a pamphlet called 'The Interest of England Stated'.[10] In it he identified the interests of all the groups who were jostling for power as selfish and against the general interest of the nation. He concluded that it was 'plain and evident' that the recall of the King was the only answer — 'he being an hereditary Prince, his private interest must be the same with that of the Nation'. He saw the events of the civil war and its aftermath as clear proof of the maxim that 'religion is the cement of government, without a publick profession of which, and maintenance of learning and ministry, atheism and disorder must need break in'.

Fell was elected Bishop of Oxford in January 1676 and consecrated in February. He remained both Dean of Christ Church and Bishop of Oxford until his death in 1686. Most contemporary and subsequent accounts of his life concentrate on his activities within the university, and give little indication of his achievements and impact as bishop, beyond general statements to the effect that he attempted too much,[11] that his excessive

---

[8] For an account of Fell's building work at Christ Church, see R. A. Beddard, 'Christ Church under John Fell', supplement to *Christ Church 1976* (published 1977).

[9] *H.M.C.*, Portland, VII, 29 (1901), 76, 114, 402.

[10] Bodl., Wood 533 (13).

[11] Anthony Wood judged that 'grasping at and undertaking too many affairs relating to the public (few of which he thoroughly effected) brought him untimely to his end'. *DNB*.

zeal made him unpopular,[12] and that his principal work was the rebuilding of the episcopal house at Cuddesdon.[13] A study of the papers that survive from the time of Fell's episcopate, chiefly among the diocesan papers, throws some light on his work as bishop and especially on Burnet's much-quoted judgement that Fell was 'a little too much heated in the matter of our disputes with the dissenters'.[14]

Fell, in common with all Anglican bishops in 1676, was anxious to deal with the problem of dissenters — men and women who chose to worship God outside the Church of England as it had been re-established in 1662. The bishops had witnessed the overthrow of the Anglican church once in their lifetimes, and saw the existence of groups of dissenters as a continuing threat to the survival of the established church. It was as difficult then as it is now to determine the exact strength of the various sects in Oxfordshire. The best general picture is given in the return made by Walter Blandford, as Bishop of Oxford, in 1669, in reply to Archbishop Sheldon's inquiries about the strength and distribution of dissent.[15] The return (printed below, pp. 40–47, from Lambeth MS. 951/1, ff. 111–13) reveals three distinct areas of nonconformist activity in the diocese. The most notable of these was a band across the north of the county of conventicles meeting in the adjacent parishes of Sibford Gower, Hook Norton, Swalcliffe, Tadmarton, Bloxham, Adderbury, and Deddington. The conventicles in the south-east of the county formed another group, all, except Warborough, adjoining the Buckinghamshire border — Thame, Aston Rowant, Lewknor, Watlington, and Henley. Those in the west of the county formed a more scattered group — Chipping Norton, Charlbury, Shipton under Wychwood, North Leigh, Wilcote, Brize Norton, and Cogges. Only Bicester had a flourishing conventicle in the north-east area, which was more noted for Catholic than for Protestant dissent. The return emphasized the strong link between the leaders of the conventicles and the Parliamentarian forces in the civil war. In Henley, Warborough, Chadlington, Hook Norton, and Tadmarton, the principal nonconformists were said to have been officers or soldiers in Cromwell's or Lambert's armies. On the whole the Anglican authorities in Oxfordshire had no

---

[12] Burnet thought 'He had much zeal for reforming abuses; and managed it perhaps with too much heat, and in too peremptory a way. But we have so little of that among us, that no wonder if such men are censured by those who love not such patterns, of such severe task masters.' *History of his own Time* (London, 1724), I, 695.

[13] *DNB*. See also J. C. Cole, 'The building of the second palace at Cuddesdon', *Oxoniensia*, XXIV (1959), 49–69.

[14] Burnet, *History of his own Time*, I, 695. For more recent general accounts of Fell, see *DNB*; H. L. Thompson, *Christ Church* (London, 1900), 82–99; Stanley Morison, *John Fell, the University Press and 'Fell' Types* (Oxford, 1967).

[15] Most of the returns were printed by G. Lyon Turner in *Early Records of Nonconformity* (London, 1911–12).

great cause for concern in the social standing of the chief supporters of the conventicles. For the most part they were reported as working men, a fellmonger in Watlington, a tobacco-cutter, a bottlemaker and a shoemaker in Warborough, a former shoemaker in Chipping Norton, a baker in Bicester, and a miller in Wilcote. Only at Cogges, near Witney, was the lord of the manor, Mr Blake,[16] said to encourage dissent; indeed the conventicle met in his house. Bray Doyly, in whose house the Quakers met in Adderbury, was lord of the manor of Adderbury West, but the return did not note his status.[17]

What must have been of greater concern to Bishop Blandford was the large number of Presbyterian and Independent clergymen, ejected from the Anglican church in 1662, who were active in his diocese, preaching at conventicles. Eight of the fifteen nonconformist ministers returned as teachers in 1669 were men of some eminence. It is not surprising that the conventicles they served were those with the largest congregations (about 300 in Henley, about 200 each in Thame, Adderbury and Cogges, and between 100 and 200 in Bicester). Of these, two, Samuel Wells and John Troughton, both lived and preached within the diocese. Wells[18] was a native of Oxford city and a graduate of Oxford university, who had, from 1644 to 1647, been a chaplain in the Parliamentary army. He became vicar of Banbury in 1648, and was of sufficiently moderate opinions to organize a protest against Parliament's proposal to put the King on trial. In 1654, he was appointed one of the commission for Oxfordshire to eject scandalous and unsuitable ministers. Deprived of his living in 1662, he continued to live in Banbury until the Five Mile Act forced him to move to Deddington. His influence was significant in the development of strong Presbyterian congregations in and around Banbury. Calamy describes him as an excellent preacher, a man 'of a cheerful disposition, of a large and liberal heart, but especially to good uses'.[19] John Troughton,[20] ejected from a fellowship at St John's College, retired to Bicester, where he kept a school. The 1669 return shows him preaching at Cogges. In 1672, he was licensed to preach in William Burnard's barn at Caversfield, and in his own house at Bicester.[21] According to Anthony Wood, who was not in the habit of flattering dissenters, Troughton was a good school-divine and metaphysician, much commended for his disputations, and respected by many conforming clergy for his wide knowledge and moderate views.[22]

---

[16] A woollen merchant from London, who had bought the manor from Sir Francis Lee in 1667, see below, p. 73, n. 404.
[17] See below, p. 44.
[18] 1614–78. For an account of him, see *DNB*.
[19] Calamy, II, 541.
[20] *c.*1637–81. For an account of him, see *DNB*.
[21] Lyon Turner, II, 827.
[22] Anthony Wood, *Athenae*, ed. Bliss, IV, 9–11.

Five eminent nonconformist clergymen preached at conventicles in Oxford diocese in 1669, but resided elsewhere. Henry Langley,[23] who preached at Cogges, had been one of the Presbyterian ministers chosen to prepare the way for the reformation of the university in 1646, by preaching in the churches of the city. He became Master of Pembroke in 1647, canon of Christ Church in 1648, and was, according to Calamy, 'a judicious, solid divine'.[24] On ejection from these posts, he retired to Tubney (just over the county boundary into Berkshire), where he kept a school. He frequently preached at private meetings in Abingdon, as well as at Cogges. In the 1670s, Langley was associated with John Troughton, Henry Cornish and Thomas Gilbert[25] in serving a dissenting congregation in the city of Oxford. According to Wood, this conventicle met in Thame Street, in the suburbs, and was frequented by scholars of the university 'out of novelty'.[26] Henry Cornish had been a canon of Christ Church until he was removed by Charles II's commissioners. He was chaplain to Sir Philip Harcourt, and preached in Oxford and occasionally about the county, as he was reported doing at Cogges in 1669.[27] In 1672 he was licensed to preach in any allowed place.[28] Sometime after the death of Troughton, he replaced him as minister to the Presbyterian congregation in Bicester, and stayed there until his death in 1698.[29] Calamy, who knew him, described him as 'a man of very generous and public spirit, sincere and pious'.[30] George Swinnock[31] was one of three nonconformist preachers resident in Buckinghamshire, who were active in Oxford diocese, chiefly in Thame. On his ejection from two Buckinghamshire livings in 1662, he lived with the family of Richard Hampden of Great Hampden, as their

---

[23] 1611–79. For an account of him, see *DNB*. His will survives as MS. Wills Berks, 94/87.
[24] Calamy, II, 59.
[25] 1613–94. An Independent, who on ejection from the vicarage of Upper Winchendon, Bucks., settled in Oxford, and preached in private houses, including that of Lord Wharton. He did not take charge of any dissenting congregation, and died in poverty. For a full account of him, see *DNB*.
[26] Anthony Wood, *Athenae*, ed. P. Bliss, IV, 406.
[27] See below, p. 47.
[28] Lyon Turner, II, 827.
[29] His will, in which he bequeathed two houses in Oxford to his daughters, and various theological works to his friends, is MS. Wills Oxon. 121/2/5. His funeral in the parish church of Bicester caused offence to White Kennett, who thought the Anglican clergyman preaching on that occasion had missed a fine opportunity to impress on his hearers the charity of the Church of England, in receiving for burial the body of one who had been 'the voice and soul of schism in that town', who 'by strength of prejudice and the force of ill example chose to serve God in a common and unhallowed barn'. He was shocked that the clergyman did not impress on the congregation the evils of dissent, or underline the fact that 'their late beloved teacher' had chosen to be buried in the parish church. [White Kennett], *Some Remarks on the Life, Death and Burial of Mr. Henry Cornish* (London, 1699).
[30] Calamy, II, 67.
[31] 1627–73. For an account of him, see *DNB*.

chaplain. He preached at conventicles in Bledlow and High Wycombe, as well as in Thame and Bicester. He published several theological treatises and sermons. Samuel Clarke[32] was, like Swinnock, living in Buckinghamshire in 1669, when he was reported preaching in Thame. On his ejection from the living of Grendon Underwood, Buckinghamshire, he was for a while with the family of Lord Wharton, then settled in Wycombe. His life's work, an annotated edition of the Bible, is a monument to 'his exact learning, singular piety and indefatiguable industry'.[33] The sermon preached at his funeral in 1701,[34] summed up the beliefs and practice of many ministers who 'for non-compliance with such rules, as (he thought) neither Christ nor his Apostles commanded or practised' found themselves deprived of their offices within the Church of England, who rather than give up their ministry, 'incessantly pursued the service of the Lord, by the press, in the pulpit, and by teaching from house to house as opportunity offered'. Robert Bennet,[35] who also preached at Thame, was, like Clarke, best known for one great work; his was *A Theological Concordance*, first published in 1657, which was in use for many generations. After his ejection from the rectory of Waddesdon, Buckinghamshire, he settled first in Aylesbury, then in Abingdon.

Edward Bagshaw,[36] who was preaching in Bicester in 1669, had been ejected from the adjoining parish of Ambrosden in 1661. Although a man of great ministerial gifts and considerable ability, he was a very different personality from the other nonconformists preaching in the diocese in 1669. They were men distinguished for their learning, piety and devotion to their flocks. Although a Student of Christ Church, who had been episcopally ordained, Bagshaw achieved a certain notoriety after the Restoration, by conspicuously linking his religious dissent with talk of political sedition. In October 1662, he was reported to be talking wildly about discontent in London, the King and his mistresses, the Queen and her cabal, and the possibility of an armed uprising. As a result of this, he was imprisoned first in the Tower, then in Southsea Castle, and was only released in November 1667.[37] His long imprisonment seems to have done little to curb his active dissent. He was reported in 1669 to be preaching in no fewer than nine conventicles — the epitome of the itinerant nonconformist — at Bicester in Oxfordshire, Westbury in Buckinghamshire, Wanlip in Leicestershire, Priors Marston and Burton Dassett in Warwickshire, and Brackley, Sulgrave, Passenham, and Towcester in his native

---

[32] 1626–1701. For an account of him, see *DNB*.
[33] Calamy, II, 105.
[34] Bodl., 11136 e.14.
[35] Died 1687. For an account of him, see *DNB*.
[36] 1629–71. For an account of him, see *DNB*.
[37] *Cal. S.P.Dom.*, 1661–62, pp. 531, 606; 1662–63, pp. 8, 461, 466, 536, 546; 1665–66, p. 191; 1667–68, p. 14.

Northamptonshire. What must to the authorities have looked like excessive zeal led to his being suspected of sedition, and imprisoned in Newgate in 1670. It is interesting to note that, of these eight eminent nonconformist ministers reported in 1669, two (Bagshaw and Swinnock) had died before Fell became bishop, three (Wells, Langley, and Troughton) died during Fell's episcopate, while Bennett, Cornish and Clarke survived him.

Archbishop Sheldon had asked for more information about the conventicles in 1669 than the place of their meeting, the standing of their principal supporters, and the names of their teachers. He also wanted to know the number of people that attended them, and what sect they belonged to. Neither question can have been easy to answer accurately. It was inevitable that most numbers given would be very approximate. In Oxford diocese, four conventicles, two at Watlington, one at Warborough, and one at Sibford Gower, are listed without any indication of their size, and two more, at Bloxham, are described as 'neither in any considerable number'. The remainder range from '20 or 30' in Chipping Norton and 'about 30' in Lewknor, Charlbury, and Chadlington, to 'about 200' in Cogges and Thame, and 'about 300' in Henley. The total, of about 1,960 people attending conventicles in the diocese in 1669, is therefore very approximate, and makes no allowance for the six conventicles where no figure is given in the return. Moreover, the number of people attending conventicles is not necessarily the same as the number of committed dissenters from the established church. Men and women might attend their parish church in the morning, take Communion once a year (an act regarded as proof of conformity), but still frequent a conventicle in the afternoon, from a desire to hear a different preacher, to enjoy a different form of worship, or just out of curiosity, like the Oxford students, who went to criticize the various preachers at the conventicle in Thame Street.[38] On the other hand, many dissenters had, from the beginning of Charles II's reign, misgivings about complete separation from the established church. Henry Cornish was reckoned to be anxious not to keep his flock 'altogether from the Church; but should sometimes set them the example of going thither himself. And he did at first resolve to begin, and end, his public exercises at such hours, as should not interfere with the solemn service of the church; but dismiss them from one place, to attend at the other'.[39] He was, like John Troughton, buried in the parish church of Bicester. Samuel Wells, ejected from the vicarage of Banbury, used to attend the parish church there, to hear the sermons of the conforming minister, although he was himself minister to the thriving

---

[38] See above, p. xvi and n. 26.
[39] [White Kennett], *Some Remarks* . . ., see above, n. 29.

dissenting congregation in the town.⁴⁰ Archdeacon Palmer of Northampton estimated that half of the attenders at conventicles in Peterborough diocese were only 'semi-separatists', who 'do yet frequent the church'.⁴¹ He also thought that the size of conventicles gave an exaggerated impression of the total number of dissenters, because the same people met in several different places.

Another attempt to discover the strength of the dissenters in the kingdom was made in 1676, when instructions went from the archbishop to all the bishops to collect information from the incumbents on the number of inhabitants, papists and nonconformists in each parish. Fell included questions to this effect in the articles of inquiry for his primary visitation.⁴² The returns handed in by the incumbents were summarized and sent on to London, where a fair copy of most of the figures for the province of Canterbury was made.⁴³ From these it appears that there were, in the parishes in ordinary jurisdiction in the diocese of Oxford, 343 Papists and 1,170 nonconformists, out of a total of 38,284 inhabitants over sixteen.⁴⁴ Such figures can only be taken as an indication of the general strength of dissent, not as a precise number of dissenters. The difficulty of defining a dissenter in the second half of the seventeenth century, and the problems inherent in deciding who, among one's parishioners did, and who did not, 'relinquish the Communion of the Church',⁴⁵ are now generally recognized. The letters to Fell from Oxfordshire clergymen in 1682, which form the major part of the text of this volume, provide interesting confirmation of these difficulties. The curate of Adderbury considered that he had in his parish 'very few indeed that wilfully and constantly absent themselves from the offices of the Church', but he was perplexed by the large number of his flock who attended the conventicle in Banbury on 'one part of the day . . . and the public workshop of God on the other'. He saw them as 'borderers betwixt two kingdomes, one can't well tell what Prince they are subject to'.⁴⁶ In listing the people who had not received Communion at Easter, the curate of Caversham grouped them into Papists, suspected Papists, Quakers, 'Dissenters and never

---

⁴⁰ V.C.H., Oxon., x, 112.
⁴¹ Northamptonshire R.O., Fermor Hesketh (Baker), MS. 708.
⁴² Bodl., C.8, 22 Linc. (19), p. 8.
⁴³ This survives in the William Salt Library (Staffordshire R.O., Salt MS. 33). An edition of the whole manuscript is shortly to be published by Dr Anne Whiteman. I am grateful to her for permission to use her figures, and for general discussion on the nature of post-Restoration dissent.
⁴⁴ For parishes in Dorchester peculiar, the return was 1,548 inhabitants, 15 Papists, 72 nonconformists; in Banbury peculiar, 1,326 inhabitants, 1 Papist, 33 nonconformists; in Thame peculiar, 1,914 inhabitants, 1 Papist, 107 nonconformists. For the two latter returns, see Queen's College, Oxford, Misc. Coll. 501.
⁴⁵ Fell's wording in his visitation articles of 1676, see above, n. 42.
⁴⁶ See below, p. 2.

came to church (except once or at most twice) these twelve months', then those who attended church 'very seldom in a morning, but never in an afternoon', 'very constantly in a morning, but seldom in the afternoon', and 'oftener in the afternoon than in the morning'. Only by devising seven different groups could he clearly describe the church-going habits of his negligent parishioners. Of all of these only two were known by him to frequent conventicles.[47] Given this variation in adherence to the established church, it would be foolish to try to ascertain an exact number of dissenters within any diocese at any point in this period. It is to the meetings of the dissenters, to their survival or disappearance as separate congregations, that we must turn, to decide on the strength of dissent in the diocese during Fell's episcopate.

Even here, the Anglican clergy had problems of definition. The 1669 return of conventicles is not at all precise in identifying the sects of the various meetings. Those at which nonconformist clergy preached were generally (and probably correctly) identified as Presbyterian, but only at Deddington was the conventicle described as simply 'Presbyterian'. Those at Thame, Chadlington, and Adderbury were considered to include Anabaptists also; at Cogges, Presbyterians and Independents joined forces; while at Bicester and Henley the conventicles were described as of separatists of all sorts, and at Kingston Blount 'Presbyterians, Independents, Quakers and Sabbatarians mixt'. Except for this last conventicle, the meetings of Quakers were by 1669 clearly identified by the authorities. The return includes Quaker conventicles at Henley, Warborough, Charlbury, Shipton under Wychwood, Adderbury, Tadmarton, Sibford Gower, and Bloxham. This fits the picture of Quaker activity in the diocese at this time drawn from their own records. A Quarterly Meeting for Oxfordshire was established in 1668, with constituent Monthly Meetings at Banbury, Warborough, and Witney, to be responsible for the various preparative meetings in the north, south, and west areas of the county.[48] Meetings of Anabaptists were identified in 1669 at Lewknor, Warborough, Hook Norton, Swalcliffe, Bloxham, and Wilcote, as well as at Thame, Watlington, and Chadlington, where they were thought to meet with the Presbyterians. The return makes special mention of Wormsley House, in Lewknor parish, the home of Colonel Adrian Scrope, where the first two meetings of the Berkshire Association of

---

[47] See below, p. 8.
[48] Of the surviving records of Oxfordshire Quakers in the second half of the seventeenth century, those of the Oxfordshire and Berkshire Quarterly Meeting are at Berks. R.O., those of the Banbury Monthly Meeting at O.R.O., and those of the Witney Monthly Meeting at present at the Friends' Meeting House in St Giles (to be transferred to the O.R.O.). For an account of the structure of the Society in the county, see E. D. Paul, 'The records of the Banbury Monthly Meeting of the Society of Friends', *Oxoniensia*, XXXI (1966), 163–65.

Baptists had met in 1652.⁴⁹ Evidence of the influence of Seventh Day Baptists is seen in the return of two Sabbatarian conventicles in Watlington and Warborough in 1669. They had probably developed as off-shoots from the strong group led by Edward Stennett in the precincts of Wallingford Castle.⁵⁰ Finally the return noted one small conventicle of Independents in Chipping Norton.

The pattern of dissent in the diocese revealed by the 1669 return can be, in part, confirmed and supplemented by a study of the licences granted under Charles II's Declaration of Indulgence in 1672.⁵¹ In this declaration, issued by virtue of the royal prerogative while Parliament was prorogued, the King suspended all the penal laws against dissenters, both Protestant and Catholic. They could now meet freely for worship, provided that they obtained licences from Whitehall for their meeting houses and their preachers. By themselves these licences do not provide a comprehensive list of dissenting congregations, because all Quakers, some Baptists and a few Congregationalists refused to apply for them, believing that the King had no more right to grant freedom in religion than he had to take it away. Licences were granted for several meeting houses in Oxford diocese in places where conventicles had been reported in 1669 — Presbyterian at Adderbury, Bicester, Deddington, Henley, and Watlington; Congregational at Chipping Norton, Henley, Thame, and Watlington; and Baptist at Finstock (in Charlbury parish). In addition, licences were granted for three Presbyterian meeting places in Banbury and for one Congregational one in Dorchester; in both parishes there is evidence of active conventicles from other sources, though neither was included in the 1669 return, perhaps because they were in peculiar jurisdiction.⁵² In Oxford city itself, where no conventicles were reported in 1669,⁵³ one Presbyterian, one Baptist and two Congregationalist houses were licensed as meeting places in 1672.

Thus the records of 1669, 1672, and 1676, with those of the Quaker quarterly and monthly meetings, show that there were several active conventicles meeting in the diocese when Fell became bishop. There were two methods open to him, as to all his colleagues on the episcopal bench, if they sought to force dissenters back into the fold of the church. Firstly, the dissenters could be prosecuted through the machinery of the

---

⁴⁹ See E. A. Payne, *The Baptists of Berkshire* (London, 1951), p. 11.
⁵⁰ Ibid., p. 47.
⁵¹ A classified summary is in Lyon Turner, III, 826–30.
⁵² The houses of William Weston, Samuel Wells and James Sutton in Banbury; that of Lawrence Overy in Dorchester. For Sutton, see D. M. Barratt, 'James Sutton — A Presbyterian Preacher', *Cake and Cockhorse*, vol. 6, no. 2 (1975), 30–32.
⁵³ Though there were certainly active groups of Quakers, Baptists, Presbyterians and Independents in the city, their meetings may well have been temporarily suppressed in 1669.

ecclesiastical courts. Churchwardens and incumbents had a duty to report to the archdeacon and bishop at their visitations all parishioners who absented themselves from their parish church or who neglected to receive Holy Communion at least once a year. These offenders were then called to answer the presentment in the ecclesiastical courts, and, on admission of the fault, or on refusal to amend their conduct, or on failure to appear to answer the charge, they could be excommunicated. Two lists which survive among the diocesan papers, one of excommunicated persons, 1661–65, and one of Popish Recusants and others who failed to attend church, c.1663–65, suggest that dissenters were vigorously pursued this way when William Paul was Bishop of Oxford.[54] Excommunication carried with it several disabilities, chiefly those of being unable to plead at law in certain cases or to act as an executor. The not infrequent requests for the sentence of excommunication to be lifted show that it was not a punishment that all regarded lightly.[55] Moreover, people who obstinately remained excommunicate for forty days could be imprisoned by the secular authorities, on a writ *de excommunicato capiendo*, a fate which afflicted several Quakers in the diocese in the 1660s.[56] Under the 1559 Act of Uniformity, churchwardens were empowered to levy a fine of 12*d*. for each week that a parishioner failed to attend his parish church. There is evidence of the enforcement of this law in Watlington in 1682 and 1683, and in Chinnor in 1685.[57]

Secondly, the church could call on the civil power to help in the task of enforcing conformity. Statutes of the reign of Elizabeth I which imposed fines and terms of imprisonment on recusants had been revived by the Long Parliament of 1661. To these acts were added the Quaker Act of 1662, the first Conventicle Act of 1664 and the Five Mile Act of 1665, which imposed heavy fines or imprisonment on more than five people who met to worship without following the Anglican forms, and forbade all non-conforming clergy from coming within five miles of any parish where they had been ministers or had held conventicles, and from any city, corporate town or parliamentary borough. The second Conventicle Act of 1670 reduced the fines on ordinary worshippers at conventicles, but increased them on preachers and owners of the houses where the conventicles met. It also provided for the goods of offenders to be

---

[54] MSS. Oxf. Dioc. c.99, ff. 237–44, c.430, ff. 38–44.

[55] For example, Edward Jennings of Oxford, St Michael, with his wife excommunicated in 1662 for not attending church, asked for absolution in 1667 (MS. Oxf. Dioc. c.9, f. 140^v); Thomas Langford of Charlbury, whose wife, daughter and two sons had just been excommunicated, asked in March 1664 for the excommunication to be lifted, and promised 'he would use his best endeavours to make them conformable to lawe' (MS. Oxf. Dioc. c.4, f.158^v).

[56] For example, Thomas Minchin of Burford, George Weston of Combe and Richard Smith of Stokenchurch, see below, pp. 54, n. 95, 61, n. 208, 65, n. 252.

[57] MS. D. D. Par. Watlington c.8, ff. 32, 43; see below, p. 11.

distrained and sold to pay the fines, and for one third of the money thus raised to go to the informer who had secured the conviction. All these penal laws were to be enforced in the civil courts by the local magistrates, who, under the second Conventicle Act, were liable to a fine of £100 if they failed to implement them. Unfortunately, the records of Oxfordshire Quarter Sessions do not survive before 1687, so no systematic study of the use of the civil magistrates to enforce religious conformity in the county can be made. Many instances of the enforcement of the penal laws can, however, be gathered from the records of the dissenters themselves.

The Five Mile Act certainly affected non-conforming clergy in the county. Henry Cornish[58] had to move from Cowley to Stanton Harcourt, and Samuel Wells[59] had to leave Banbury for Deddington. Another ejected minister, Francis Hubbard[60] was imprisoned for six months in Oxford in 1665, 'being taken preaching in a private house'.[61] Stephen Ford, ejected from the vicarage of Chipping Norton, was so harrassed by the civil authorities in the town, that his life was considered in danger, and he fled to London.[62] Samuel Birch, ejected vicar of Bampton, was 'perpetually molested' and in 1666 imprisoned for holding conventicles.[63] Among lay dissenters, the Quakers probably suffered most,[64] for they refused to pay tithes or church rates, would not compromise by occasionally attending their parish churches, and would not take any oath, such as the oath of allegiance which was frequently tendered to them, as a test of their loyalty to the King.[65] Thomas Gilpin of Warborough was imprisoned for seven weeks in 1660 for refusing to take the oath of allegiance.[66] Giles Tidmarsh was in Oxford gaol from 1661 to 1673;[67] with Thomas Minchin, Thomas Reeve, George Weston and Thomas Hadduck, he petitioned the bishop for release in 1667 or 1668.[68] All had been in prison for six or seven years. In the event, most had to wait for the King's Declaration of Indulgence in 1672 before they were freed. Shortly after this petition was sent, Thomas Reeve of Great Tew died in prison[69] — the only Quaker whose death in

---

[58] See below, p. 66, n. 277.
[59] See below, p. 55, n. 111.
[60] See below, p. 61, n. 211.
[61] *Calamy Revised*, p. 280.
[62] *Calamy Revised*, p. 206.
[63] *Calamy Revised*, p. 56; see below, p. 50, n. 24.
[64] See below, pp. 70, n. 350, 71, n. 375.
[65] It is noticeable in the records of the ecclesiastical courts, that the Quakers usually gave their reasons for dissenting in plain terms — e.g., Thomas Fletcher of Middle Barton, who in 1663 refused to attend his parish church because 'he doth not take that meeting house for the parish to be a church, nor doth he allow of the prayers there, nor will he promise to go to that meeting house' (MS. Oxf. Dioc. c.6, f. 30ᵛ).
[66] See below, p. 70, n. 350.
[67] See below, p. 62, n. 215.
[68] MS. Oxf. Dioc. c.650, f. 68a.
[69] Besse, *Sufferings*, I, 569.

prison in the county is recorded. Quaker meetings in Oxford, Milton under Wychwood and Brize Norton were broken up in 1660 and most of the men were sent to Oxford gaol.[70] Seven men were taken out of the Burford meeting and imprisoned in 1662. Nine people were removed from a meeting in a house in Cogges in 1666 and committed by the justices to the 'house of correction' for one month.[71] In Banbury the Quakers suffered numerous imprisonments, fines, and forcible breaking up of their meetings.[72] For the county as a whole, Besse gives a long list of imprisonments, fines and distresses on goods throughout the period 1660 to 1689.[73] An example of the levying of fines under the second Conventicle Act is recorded in the 'Sufferings Book' of the Oxfordshire Quakers.[74] Two justices, John Gower of Weald and John Gunn of Clanfield, broke up a meeting in the house of John Wheeler, a bodice-maker, in Alvescot in February 1675. The following month the constables and churchwarden came with a warrant from the justices and took from Wheeler goods (including the tools of his trade) worth £16. All the others who attended the meeting were fined 5s. or had goods to that value taken away. Two wealthy members, William Warwick and William Wise, each had goods worth £10 taken away, to pay the fines of those who were too poor to have sufficient goods of their own distrained.[75]

A tradition of persecution of Baptists in Oxfordshire has also survived, though in more general terms. The most notorious example was the case of Joseph Davis, a Baptist mercer of Chipping Norton, and a 'zealous and pious preacher', who had all his goods confiscated and was imprisoned in Burford gaol in 1660. In 1661, after Venner's insurrection, and again in 1662 and in 1663, he was imprisoned in Oxford. He was held there for ten years in all, having been freed temporarily in 1665 to attend his wife's deathbed. On being set at liberty at the King's Declaration of Indulgence, he wisely moved to London, where he prospered as a linen merchant, and died in 1706.[76] Josiah Diston,[77] a leading Baptist in Chipping Norton, left a manuscript account of their sufferings, written in 1707, which was used in 1739 in Thomas Crosby's *History of the English Baptists*.[78] Diston wrote in general terms of meetings being broken up, of appearances before hostile justices, and of the infliction of heavy fines and long terms of

[70] Stephen Allott, *Friends in Oxford* (Oxford, 1952); Besse, *Sufferings*, I, 567.
[71] Besse, *Sufferings*, I, 569–70.
[72] *V.C.H., Oxon.*, x, 109–10.
[73] Besse, *Sufferings*, I, 566–76.
[74] Bound in a volume of Sufferings of the Vale of White Horse meeting, 1673–1722.
[75] See below, p. 50 and nn. 31, 33,
[76] A. C. Underwood, *A History of the English Baptists* (London, 1947), 99–100; Eileen Meades, *History of Chipping Norton* (Oxford, 1949), p. 49.
[77] See below, p. 70, n. 360.
[78] Crosby, II, 258.

imprisonment. Only when he came to supply 'testimonies of God's dislike of such proceedings, by his hand of providence stretched out against some of the chief persecutors and informers against the Protestant Dissenters in Oxfordshire' did he give much detail. These instances of awful death, extinction of long-established families, and failure in business were understandably popular at the time, and provide rather bizarre, and certainly biased evidence of the attitude of Oxfordshire justices to dissent in the county.

The intensity of prosecution of dissenters under the penal laws varied enormously from area to area of the country and even of a single county, and from year to year within the period from the Restoration to the Toleration Act of 1689. The attitude of both the King and Parliament to dissent vacillated, and public opinion was easily swayed by fears that dissenters were rebels involved in Venner's insurrection of 1661, in the Rye House Plot of 1683, and in Monmouth's Rebellion of 1685 on the one hand, or by the panic of the supposed Popish Plot of 1678 on the other. The belief that religious dissent was closely allied with civil insurrection had been reinforced by the experiences of the civil war and Commonwealth. It was on this belief that the use of the civil power against dissenters was founded; but no systematic persecution along the lines of that of Huguenots in France during the 1680s was possible in an England which conspicuously lacked the strong centralized administration that France enjoyed. The English central government relied on the justices of the peace in each county to enforce the penal laws against dissenters, but it lacked any system for controlling their actions. Some magistrates in Oxfordshire seem to have been zealous in performing this duty. Josiah Diston listed Lord Falkland, the Lord Lieutenant, Sir Thomas Peniston, Deputy Lieutenant, Sir William Moreton and Sir Thomas Roe as 'bitter persecutors of the Dissenters, employing their whole power to ruin them', who, 'by some blast of providence', came to be ruined themselves, 'their estates sold and most of their families extinct'. As we are dependent on the evidence provided by the persecuted themselves, it is impossible to decide if these justices were, as Diston maintained, more tolerant of criminals than of dissenters. What we can conclude is that some Oxfordshire magistrates certainly put the penal laws into force. Lord Saye and Sele, of Broughton Castle, had a similar reputation in the Banbury area. He evicted Quakers from cottages on his estates; irritated by what he considered the insolence of two Quakers who refused to take off their hats to him, he had them committed to gaol; he was active in inflicting fines and imprisonment on those who attended Quaker meetings. Lord Saye and Sele's pamphlet, with the Quakers' reply,[79] provides a clear

---

[79] William Fiennes, Lord Saye and Sele. *Folly and Madnesse made manifest* and *The Quakers Reply* (Oxford, 1659, 1660). Bodl., Wood 645 (13).

example of the lack of common ground between Anglican and nonconformist. The Quakers saw him as a persecutor of men who only met together to worship God. He saw the Quakers as heretics and potential 'Levellers' and maintained that he was not a persecutor 'of their persons but of their intollerable pride'. He justified the eviction of Quaker tenants, on the grounds that his cottages should be let 'to men that will serve God with me'.

In 1669, the Thame conventicle was reported as having moved into Buckinghamshire when the Oxfordshire justices took action against it.[80] The letters to Fell from Oxfordshire clergymen in 1682 also supply some evidence of the activities of the justices. Captain Henry Bertie, younger brother of the Earl of Abingdon, and Giles Gregory of Caversham took steps to ensure that the constable of Aston Rowant did his duty in reporting dissenters to the justices.[81] Gregory, with Sir Henry Allnutt, had so enforced the penal laws in the south-east of the county, that some of the dissenters in Lewknor had left the area, declaring it to be 'the warmest corner' of 'the persecuted Shire of England'.[82] On the other hand, in 1684, Joseph Ball of Bloxham appealed to the Secretary of State for allowance of his charges in informing against three notorious Quakers, who had not been prosecuted at the Quarter Sessions, 'the justices being so favourable that many Quakers come to live in Oxfordshire because they are not prosecuted'.[83] Some Oxfordshire justices may well have shared the scruples of Edmund Verney of Claydon, Buckinghamshire, who, in 1682, disliked signing the presentments of Papists and dissenters, 'hating to do anything like an informer, though never so legally'.[84] The petition of Joan Reeve to Bishop Blandford in 1667 provides indirect evidence that at times the justices were merciful. She asked that her Quaker husband, who had been in Oxford gaol for three years and was very old and weak, might be allowed to return home, so long as he reported to every general Quarter Sessions — an arrangement that had been made in other similar cases.[85] It seems that this request was not granted, and that her husband died in gaol.[86] On occasion, the severity of the justices could be thwarted by lesser officials, as happened in Witney in 1675. The constables of Bampton distrained goods and levied fines imposed by the justices' warrant, on Quakers who had attended a meeting in Alvescot, but those of Witney 'being more moderate did not distraine', except on one offender.[87]

[80] See below, p. 40.
[81] See below, p. 5.
[82] See below p. 26.
[83] *Cal. S.P.Dom.*, 1683/4, p. 384.
[84] M. M. Verney, *Memoirs of the Verney Family*, IV (London, 1899), 178.
[85] MS. Oxf. Dioc. c.650, f. 66.
[86] See above, p. xxiii.
[87] See above, p. xxiv.

There is little evidence about Fell's attitude to the use of the penal laws against dissenters. There is no reason to doubt that he shared the widely-held view that obstinate dissenters should be prosecuted.[88] What is clear is that he was not content to rely on coercion alone. He believed that improvements in the standards of the established church were a pre-requisite of winning them back. There is much evidence, both in his published works and in his correspondence, to show that Fell placed great emphasis on the importance of the parochial clergy in combating dissent and in strengthening the Anglican church. He thought that the example of diligent and committed clergymen could not help but reclaim the dissenting and the negligent. As early as 1661, in describing the activities of Henry Hammond as rector of Penshurst, Fell wrote of him as a model for all to follow:

in the discharge of his ministerial function, he satisfied not himself in diligent and constant preaching only; (a performance wherein some of late have phancied all religion to consist) but much more conceived himself obliged to the offering up the solemn daily sacrifice of prayer for his people, administring the Sacraments, relieving the poor, keeping hospitality, reconciling of differences amongst neighbours, visiting the sick, catechising the youth.[89]

Fell saw the provision to the livings in his diocese of men who would reach this high standard, as a pre-condition of the health, if not the survival of the established church. This was not an easy matter for any bishop to control. As Dean of Christ Church, Fell had the advantage of being, with the Chapter, patron of several livings in his own diocese.[90] A letter in which Fell thanked the Lord Keeper for asking his advice on the suitability of a candidate who had been recommended for the living of St Clement's in Oxford, emphasizes the fact that most patrons would not bother to consult the bishop. Fell considered that this conduct proved the Lord Keeper to be a true patron of the church, 'which is concerned in nothing more then that good men should be entrusted with the care of souls'.[91] Many of the clergy of Oxfordshire throughout the ten years of his episcopate would not, of course, have been instituted by Fell; and some might well have been survivors of the troubled times of the civil war. That Fell could be cautious in his dealings with his clergy is revealed in a letter to Sancroft in July 1684, an answer to the archbishop's inquiry about the suitability of the curate of Beckley for preferment. Fell had noticed, at his

---

[88] Cf. below, p. xxxvii.
[89] John Fell, *The Life of the most learned, reverend and pious Dr H. Hammond* (London, 1661), pp. 9–10.
[90] For example, Black Bourton, Brize Norton, Cassington, Caversham, Chalgrove, Cowley, Oxford, St Mary Magdalen, Pyrton, South Stoke, Spelsbury, Westwell, and Wroxton.
[91] MS. Top. Oxon. d.314, ff. 109–10; Feb. 1682/3.

primary visitation, that the curate, Robert Hawkins, had defective letters of orders, 'but considering that my predecessors had bin satisfied concerning them, and that in the ill times, men were put to great streits, to obtain episcopal ordination, I past over that blot.'[92] This suggests that by 1676 Fell had learned the wisdom of waiting on events, and of not being over-zealous in pursuing his aims — as he wrote in 1683, he had 'often seen business spoild by striving to do it too effectually'.[93]

Fell, in common with many of his contemporaries, saw another cause of the growth of dissent in the holding of livings in plurality. As Fell included among the duties of the parochial clergy, the conducting of prayers in church daily, regular preaching, the administration of the sacrament once a month, visiting the sick, and rigorous catechizing of the young people, it is not surprising that he considered no man capable of adequately serving more than one parish. In a letter to Sancroft of 20 June 1683, Fell described the granting of dispensations to hold more than one living as 'fatal to the interest of the church', and gave as an example a dispensation granted to a Mr Corpson, 'whereby I expect that two parishes will be given up to fanaticisme and the negligence of the cheapest Curats than (sic) can be found'.[94] Anxious to counter the growth of dissent in Hook Norton, Fell, in 1682, suspended Edward Jennings, who was curate of that town and of Great Rollright, and in 1683 replaced him in Hook Norton with a man whom he had himself recently ordained. He was also concerned that the poor value of some livings made them unattractive to men of ability. An interesting example of the improvement of the value of a living in the diocese during Fell's episcopate is to be found in a letter from the Dean and Chapter of Gloucester to the Lord Chancellor, asking him to present Edward Redrobe to the vicarage of Chipping Norton in 1683.[95] The letter explained that the living was so poor that it had been vacant for twenty years, though the services of a clergyman had sometimes been procured for the parish by those inhabitants who could afford to pay one. The Dean and Chapter had decided to improve the stipend so that a good man could be appointed to take care of the large parish. It seems very likely that Fell had instigated this move, in an attempt to check the

---

[92] MS. Tanner 32, f. 101. In fact Fell had to suspend Hawkins later for 'more visible failings in morality and conversation'; but had restored him to the living on receiving a certificate of his penitence and reformation from his parishioners, only to discover that they had signed the certificate and not made any further complaints for fear that his large family, deprived of his income, should become a burden on the parish. Fell also considered Hawkins profoundly ignorant. It is not surprising that he began his letter to Sancroft, 'I have reason not to put any stop to Mr. Hawkins preferment, if it will occasion his remove out of this Diocese', but honesty prevented him from getting rid of a problem at someone else's expense.

[93] MS. Montagu d.13, f. 41.

[94] MS. Tanner 34, f. 48.

[95] See D. M. Barratt, 'Chipping Norton vicarage in 1683', *Oxoniensia*, x (1945), 105–6.

growth of the two thriving conventicles in this important market town. Fell also took steps to improve the way the cure was served in the borough of Woodstock. In 1738, the vicar of Bladon reported that he lived in Woodstock, although it was only a chapelry in his parish, 'in an House built by . . . Bp. Fell . . . to draw the Rector of Blayden to reside at Woodstock, and to induce him by such residence to perform full service in their Chapel'.[96] Fell drew the attention of Archbishop Sancroft to the problem of the town of Abingdon, 'for trade, wealth and faction, the most considerable of any in this part of England', which, because of the poor value of the living, was always ill-supplied with a minister.[97] Although it was not in his diocese, he suggested a plan for improving the minister's salary and attracting an able man to the post, as 'the only way to reform that numerous and disaffected people'. Seth Ward, Bishop of Salisbury, in whose diocese Abingdon lay, was similarly concerned — 'To keep his diocese in conformity, he took great care to settle able ministers in the great Market and Borough Towns, as Reading, Abingdon, Newbery, the Devizes, Warminster etc.'.[98]

Letters from laymen to Fell echo his views on the fundamental importance of the provision of diligent men to prevent the growth of dissent in the parishes. Robert Atkyns wrote from Stow on the Wold on 26 August 1683, about the living of Lower Swell in Gloucestershire, of which the Dean and Chapter of Christ Church were patrons. He begged Fell to provide them with a good minister, giving as his reasons:

We seldome have any Communion and not till wee invite our Minister (Mr. Callow) to afford it us. Wee have some hasty praiers in the morning every Sonday, and a few notes read to us in the afternoon for Mr. Callowe is minister too of Stow, and is in haste still to ride away from us thither, and it is no wonder if of those few that belong to us some are Quakers and some Anabaptists, and very few of the rest care for coming to church.[99]

The inhabitants of Stokenchurch asked Fell, as bishop, to provide them with a curate of their own. Since the removal of their last curate, the vicar of Aston Rowant (in which parish Stokenchurch was a chapel of ease) had served the cure himself, instead of paying someone else to do it, as he had in the past, and they feared 'he will starve both his flock at home and us also (the places being two miles or more distant). And moreover he is a man of a weak constitution.' They added the specific complaint that four weeks previously no one had come at the usual time to read divine service, 'which drives our congregation to other places, and which makes

---

[96] *Secker Visitation*, pp. 18–19.
[97] One an undated draft, MS. Rawl. D.317, f. 268, and one dated 26 June 1683, MS. Tanner 34, f. 55.
[98] Walter Pope, *The Life of . . . Seth, Lord Bishop of Salisbury* (London, 1697), p. 67.
[99] MS. Rawl. D.399, f. 279.

us much feare, we shall have a factious people amongst us'.[100] Their petition was endorsed by Fell with the name of the man who became their curate in 1681.

These illustrations of Fell's attitude to his clergy and to the problem of dissent are isolated examples, gathered from the scattered remains of his correspondence. A clearer indication of both is to be found in the papers which survive concerning his visitations of his diocese. It was by formal visitation that the bishop could discover for himself the state of affairs in the parishes of his diocese. Traditionally, visitations by the bishop in person took place every three years, and the incumbents and churchwardens would be called to give an account of the condition of their parishes. Fell held visitations in 1676, 1679, 1682, and 1685; characteristically, he gave notice of his primary visitation within six weeks of his consecration.[101] Printed *Articles of Visitation and Enquiry exhibited to the ministers, Church-wardens and Side-men of every parish* are extant for his visitations of 1676[102] and 1682,[103] but the presentments made by the incumbents and churchwardens in reply to these questions do not survive.[104]

The printed articles contain the usual inquiries about the physical condition of the churches, churchyards, and parsonages, the orthodoxy and diligence of the ministers, the beliefs and behaviour of the parishioners, the conduct of the parish clerks, sextons, and ecclesiastical officers, and the licensing of schoolmasters, physicians, surgeons, and midwives. It is clear from other material in the diocesan papers that Fell used his visitations, and especially that of 1682, to discover as exactly as he could the extent of dissent in the diocese. This concern in 1682 may well have been influenced by the political events of the three years which had passed since his previous visitation. In Oxford, as elsewhere throughout the country, fears of a Popish plot to overthrow the established government and church had encouraged the growth of a party determined to exclude the Catholic Duke of York from succession to the throne. Many dissenters had seen in this policy a hope of toleration for themselves and had supported it. Although the university remained loyal to the King's policy of upholding his brother's right to succeed to the throne, both the city of Oxford and Oxfordshire returned Whig members of Parliament in the elections of 1679 and 1681. The Duke of Monmouth visited Oxford in 1680, and, amid public rejoicing and in the presence of the members of

[100] MS. Oxf. Dioc. c.650, ff. 25–26.
[101] MS. Oxf. Dioc. c.148, no. 22.
[102] Bodl., C. 8. 22 Linc. (19).
[103] A copy is in the Library at Christ Church.
[104] The series of churchwardens' presentments for Oxfordshire parishes in ordinary jurisdiction begins in 1730.

Parliament of the city and county, was made a freeman of the city.[105] It was against this background that Fell sought in 1682 to obtain more precise information about dissenters in his diocese, and to win some of them back to the church. Thirty-five letters to Fell (in Bodl., MSS. Oxford Diocesan Papers c.430, fols. 1–36 and c.650, fol. 27), dated between April and September 1682, from incumbents of Oxfordshire parishes reveal that the bishop made a verbal request to his clergy at this visitation to furnish him with details of dissent. The information provided in these letters illustrates both the attitude of the bishop and the parochial clergy to dissenters, and the relationship between the bishop and his clergy.

No copy of Fell's charge to the clergy at this visitation has come to light, but the letters themselves give a fairly precise indication of his instructions. From them it is clear that Fell asked for much more than a note of the number of dissenters in each parish or a list of their names. Henry Gregory, rector of Middleton Stoney, started his letter with a paraphrase of the bishop's request, that the clergy

should have recourse to the severall houses or habitations of such recusants and dissenters, and there offer themselves and be ready to confer and discourse with the said recusants and dissenters concerning those principles of religion and parts of divine worship, wherin they dissent from the orders of the Church of England by law established, and to endeavour by whatsoever powerfull arguments to perswade and reduce them to a conformity with the said lawes.[106]

From the letter of Richard Evans, rector of Hethe, we learn that Fell asked for a written account of the clergy's efforts to be delivered to him 'by or before the first day of August next'.[107]

Fell clearly hoped that his clergy would be able, by force of argument, to win some of the dissenters back into the established church. The previous year he had himself had published, in pamphlet form, a translation of St Cyprian's discourse 'Of the Unity of the Church', which the title-page described as 'most usefull for allaying the present heats, and reconciling the differences among us'.[108] In his preface, Fell compared the Christian church of St Cyprian's day, enfeebled by the schism of Novatian,[109] as it tried to resist the persecution of the Emperor Decius, with the Anglican church of his own day, weakened by the schism of the Protestant dissenters,

---

[105] C. E. Whiting, *Studies in English Puritanism, 1660–1688* (London, 1931), pp. 396–97.
[106] See below, p. 26; cf. the note made in the record of the visitation of Thomas Turner, Archdeacon of Essex, in 1684, that the curate of Hockley is 'to have discourse with' the seven Anabaptists in his parish. *Transactions of the Essex Archaeological Society*, xx (1930–31), 229.
[107] See below, p. 21.
[108] Bodl., Pamph. C. 154(9); printed at Oxford, 1681.
[109] On Novatianism, see *The Oxford Dictionary of the Christian Church*, ed. F. L. Cross and E. A. Livingstone (2nd edition, Oxford, 1974), p. 984.

when it was being attacked by the Catholics. He had expressed similar sentiments in a sermon preached before the House of Lords on 22 December 1680, urging all Protestants to forget their differences and to unite against 'the inundation of Papal Tyranny which is now ready to devour them'.[110] Fell hoped that St Cyprian's arguments in favour of unity would carry more weight, because their author, having died over fourteen hundred years before, could not be accused, as so many in the controversies of Charles II's reign could, of being biased by personal interest. The letters of George Ashwell, rector of Hanwell, and Richard Parr, curate of Ibstone, show how Fell envisaged his pamphlet being used in the attempt to reduce the number of dissenters. Ashwell delivered to some of the dissenters in his parish 'that discourse of St. Cyprian concerning the unity of the church which your Lordship caused to be translated into English, and then sent hither (as to other parishes of your diocess)'.[111] Parr read St Cyprian's tract to his congregation, having previously sent word about the parish that he had 'something to communicate to them from their Bishop'.[112]

Most of the incumbents took care to inform their bishop in their letters that they had obeyed his command to confer with the dissenters in their parishes. Two letters suggest that Fell was concerned not only with active dissenters, but also with those who were negligent in attending church and receiving Holy Communion. Peter Shelley gave notice in Caversham that he would administer the Sacrament on Whit Sunday, and told his parishioners that he had a strict charge to send to the bishop an account of all who had not received Communion at Easter and neglected to do so at Whitsun.[113] The list which Shelley gave in his letter, of those who did not receive Communion on either occasion, is more detailed than any other that survives in this group. Jeremiah Wheate, whose parish of Deddington contained active groups of Presbyterians and Anabaptists, 'gave the Sacrament... according to your command when I was last to wait upon your Lordship, and we were but nine in all'.[114] It seems likely that Fell's instructions about testing conformity in this way were not given in general at his visitation, but in private, to individual incumbents who had particular problems. Fell's desire to strengthen the Church of

---

[110] Bodl., Pamph. C. 151 (7); printed at Oxford, 1680.
[111] See below, p. 18.
[112] See below, p. 23.
[113] See below, p 7; cf. the similar instructions given at the archdeacon's visitation in 1683 to the churchwardens in several Essex parishes about presenting those who did not receive Communion during the year, and especially the note at Nazeing, that the rector is to administer Holy Communion at Michaelmas, after which the churchwardens are to report those who did not receive it then or at Easter or at Whitsun. *Transactions of the Essex Archaeological Society*, xix (1927–30), 273–76.
[114] See below, p. 14.

England by reclaiming those guilty of schism and negligence, and his belief in the power of informed discussion to achieve this end, are both very clearly illustrated in this group of letters.

It is impossible to tell whether these thirty-five letters represent the total response of Oxfordshire clergy to their bishop's commands, but it seems unlikely that a man of Fell's energy and zeal would have let the matter rest there. About 190 clergymen were called to the visitation in 1682, which took place in five sessions at Chipping Norton, Henley on Thames, Oxford, Witney, and Bicester, on 20 April, 11 and 12 May, 11 and 15 June.[115] The majority of the clergy's letters about dissent are dated during June and July. The surviving letters include seven (for Chastleton, Cornwell, Islip, Middleton Stoney, Mongewell, Salford, and Woodeaton)[116] which reported that there were no dissenters in their parishes; so Fell did not only keep those letters which suggested that action needed to be taken. It is possible, of course, that many more incumbents ignored Fell's request for a *written* account, and, like Robert Parsons, curate of Adderbury, gave 'a more particular account' in person[117] when they visited Oxford. Edward Tyrer, vicar of Clanfield, assumed that as the names of the dissenters had been given in at the visitation, he did not need to repeat them in his letter, though he went on to give one Quaker's reasons for not attending church.[118] Other incumbents, having nothing to add to the presentment made at the visitation, may not have bothered to write a letter to that effect. It is clear from other papers which survive among the records of the diocese, and are discussed below, that Fell did receive and make note of more information about dissent in Oxfordshire than was sent to him in this group of letters.

Many more dissenters than are named in these letters are listed in Fell's 'diocese book' — a small vellum-bound volume, in which he kept a note of matters concerning the state of the diocese.[119] Each parish which came under the bishop's jurisdiction[120] was allotted a page or half-page in the volume, with the name of the incumbent, and sometimes the name of the patron and the value of the living, at the head. The parishes are arranged in roughly alphabetical order under the deaneries of Oxford, Cuddesdon, Witney, Woodstock, Chipping Norton, Deddington, Bicester, Henley, and Aston. The headings were drawn up by Fell in 1682, and the notes under them contain information handed in at the visitations of 1682 and 1685 (the former usually on slips of paper which have since been pasted

---

[115] Visitation call book, MS. Oxf. Dioc. d.20, ff. 3–18.
[116] See below, pp. 11, 13, 24, 26, 27, 28, and 31.
[117] See below, p. 2.
[118] See below, p. 12.
[119] MS. Oxf. Dioc. d.708.
[120] That is, all parishes in the county except those in the peculiar jurisdiction of Banbury, Thame, and Dorchester.

in). In 1682 Fell listed, usually by name, about 337 Protestant dissenters, 108 Catholic dissenters and 92 'absenters'; in 1685, the totals were 303, 98, and 79. His diocese book provides clear evidence of the interest Fell took in the problem of dissent.

A further indication of this concern, and of the action which it led Fell to take, survives in a list of queries which he drew up after his visitation in 1682.[121] Answers to most of the questions survive, in the hand of Timothy Halton, Archdeacon of Oxford from 1675 to 1704.[122] These show Fell's attempt to deal with the conventicles in which the dissenters met, and to identify and take proceedings against their leaders. Thus he inquired if Samuel Pack continued to hold a conventicle in Burford, 'that if he does he may be proceeded against according to law'; to whom the meeting-house in Witney belonged; who taught the dissenters in Charlbury; whether Bray Doyly and Thomas Whately still kept conventicles in Adderbury, and if conventicles still met in Chipping Norton, Heyford, and Aston Rowant. He was suspicious of *'omnia bene'* returns made by the churchwardens of Henley and Witney, where conventicles were known to meet. At his archidiaconal visitation, Timothy Halton managed to discover the answer to many of the bishop's queries. He reported that Samuel Pack continued to preach at Burford; that an unknown woman taught the Quakers at Charlbury; that the conventicles had ceased to meet at Heyford and Aston Rowant. No one had appeared at his visitation from Henley or Adderbury, and his silence on Chipping Norton suggests a similar lack of information. These two documents show that Fell tried, with the help of a vigorous archdeacon, to supplement the presentments made at his own visitation. In the same way, the letters from the clergy reveal that he made a direct appeal to them, when he was dissatisfied with the returns about dissent made by the churchwardens.

It is apparent that Fell endeavoured to collect exact information about dissenters through the normal machinery of his own and his archdeacon's visitations. He kept a note of their names in his diocese book, and, where he thought it appropriate, encouraged the prosecution of ringleaders. For example, he asked Halton to discover which of the Burford dissenters presented at his visitation 'are most fit to be made examples'.[123] Proceedings were then instituted in the archdeacon's court against the two preachers at the conventicle, Samuel Pack and Joshua Brooks, and they were both excommunicated in December 1682.[124] Another list, in Halton's hand, of matters which came to light at his visitation in 1683,

---

[121] MS. Oxf. Dioc. b.68, ff. 9–10; printed below, pp. 33–35.
[122] MS. Oxf. Dioc. b.68, ff. 11–12; printed below, pp. 35–36.
[123] See below, p. 33.
[124] MS. Archd. pprs. Oxon. c.121, f. 54.

survives among the diocesan papers.[125] It consists mainly of the numbers of dissenters presented in each parish, and is further evidence of Fell's continuing application to the problem of dissent in his diocese. In April 1684, a large number of people, most of them dissenters, were excommunicated for not appearing to answer charges against them.[126] On the whole, the records of the ecclesiastical courts in Oxford do not suggest that there was any marked difference in the numbers of dissenters prosecuted during Fell's episcopate and those of his predecessors since the Restoration.[127] As we have seen, there is, on the contrary, much evidence to suggest that Fell looked to more constructive methods of combating dissent. He thought that the number of dissenters would be reduced by convincing them of the evils of schism, and by the stricter application of the Anglican clergy to their parochial duties. It is interesting, though idle, to speculate whether these letters of 1682, revealing as they do the entrenched positions of most dissenters and Anglican clergymen, shook Fell's faith in the methods he advocated.

There is more than a note of disillusion in his charge to the clergy at his visitation in 1685:[128]

I need not tell you in what condition the Church now is, assaulted by the furious malice of Papists on the one hand and Fanaticks on the other, and, amidst the machinations of those who are zealous for a sect or party, more fatally attempted by the licentiousness and sloth of those who are indifferent to any or opposite to all.
...
If at any time I press my Brethren of the Clergy, to labour the reduction of the Dissenters, I am told, they are perverse and proud, and will not hear, will not be treated with. If I require a constant diligence in offering the daily sacrifice of Prayer for the people, at least at those returns which the Church enjoins, the usual answer is, they are ready to do their duty, but the people will not be prevailed with to join with them. If I call for Catechizing, it is said the Youth are backward and have no mind to come, and parents and masters are negligent to send them. If I insist on frequent Sacraments, the indevotion of the people is objected; they are not willing to communicate or they are not fit. And so when the Minister has thoroughly accused his flock, he thinks he has absolved himself, his Church becomes a *Sine-Cure*; and because others forbear to do their duty, there remains none for him to do.

Of the thirty-four incumbents who wrote to Fell in 1682 in answer to his request, seven were able to report that there were no dissenters in their

---

[125] MS. Oxf. Dioc. b.68, f.6; printed below, pp. 37–39.
[126] MS. Archd. pprs. Oxon. c.121, f. 28. They included ten from Bloxham, five from Epwell, six from Milcombe, twenty-eight from Hook Norton, seven from South Newington, five from Wigginton, and seven from Great Tew.
[127] Robert Skinner, 1660–63; William Paul, 1663–65; Walter Blandford, 1665–71; Nathaniel Crewe, 1671–74 and Henry Compton, 1674–75.
[128] MS. Tanner 31, ff. 156–57; printed in *The Student or the Oxford Monthly Miscellany*, no. 1 (Oxford, 1750), 8–10.

parishes.[129] Of the remainder, twenty-two had visited the dissenters, to discuss with them their reasons for refusing to conform. Only eight of these had much hope of their efforts bearing fruit in the return of the separatists to the Anglican church. George Ashwell, rector of Hanwell, believed that his private discourses and admonitions had done more good than his public sermons.[130] Nathaniel Collier had been surprised by the willingness of the three Anabaptists in Duns Tew to listen to his arguments on the sinfulness of separation, and now had hopes of winning them all back.[131] Robert Vicaris had had little success with the four dissenters in Spelsbury, but was 'not out of hopes of reclaiming two of them'.[132] Nicholas Page had secured promises of a return to church from some in Bloxham who had absented themselves for many years.[133] Richard Manning, vicar of Chalgrove, was able to report that one dissenter (a Roman Catholic) had been 'through my endeavours reclaimed, and brought to a compleat conformity to the prasent establish'd lawes'.[134] Thomas Reynolds, vicar of Aston Rowant, thought that two of the chief dissenters in his parish had been persuaded to return to church.[135] Edward Tyrer had secured a promise to conform from one Papist in Clanfield, as had John Beckingham from three women dissenters in Enstone.[136]

Most of the other incumbents reported that the dissenters were so set in their ways that argument would not move them, though few were as honest as John Bayly, rector of Fringford, who confessed that the fault might lie in himself. He wrote to his bishop that he lacked the 'perswasive faculty' needed to succeed in discussion.[137] As one would expect, the one nonconformist minister mentioned in these letters — Thomas Whately — was not to be convinced by the arguments of the incumbent of Deddington.[138] Men who felt strongly enough to secede from the Anglican church when it was re-established, to give up their livings because they disagreed with the government, discipline or liturgy of that church, were not likely to be won back into the fold easily twenty years later. The Quakers and Anabaptists were found by most of the incumbents to hold fast to their own beliefs, to be 'blinde and incorrigibl', 'so ignorant and obstinate, that 'tis in vain to offer any thing to their consideration'.[139]

---

[129] See above, p. xxxviii and n. 116.
[130] See below, p. 19.
[131] See below, p. 15.
[132] See below, p. 29.
[133] See below, p. 6.
[134] See below, p. 7.
[135] See below, p. 4.
[136] See below, pp. 12, 16.
[137] See below, p. 17.
[138] See below, p. 13.
[139] At Bampton and Bloxham, see below, pp. 5, 6.

Jeremiah Wheate found that the Quakers of Deddington 'insted of reasoning did nothing but cavill'.[140] At Drayton, near Banbury, Adam Morton thought the Quakers and Anabaptists could find little or nothing to say in support of their opinions, 'yet they are willfull'.[141] Hugh Boham wrote that the two dissenting families in Harpsden were 'unreformable and fit for no other remedy, but to be sent to the Hospital of St. Jacomo in Rome', which dealt with those suffering from incurable diseases.[142] Richard Evans, rector of Hethe, summed up the attitude of many of his colleagues when he wrote 'men are soe wedded to their dogmaticall humors, tho' never soe erronious, that the clergie may time after time admonish, and perswade in vaine, and find litle or noe remedy or amendment'.[143]

Many of the clergy felt that their own efforts would be of no avail with the individual dissenters in their parishes, until the civil magistrates dealt with the conventicles, as they were empowered to do under the second Conventicle Act.[144] They believed that the continued existence of such meetings not only strengthened the position of existing dissenters, but also encouraged others to join them. This was particularly true in the area around Banbury, where conventicles of all sects had flourished since the early 1660s. The Quaker and Presbyterian meetings in Adderbury were considered by the curate there to be the main cause of his problems. He felt powerless to do much good while the magistrates in the area did nothing to suppress the conventicles. The incumbents of Enstone and Drayton felt similarly helpless without the co-operation of the civil power. The latter wrote to Fell, 'unles the conventicles be suppressed, I feare the people will never be brought to any good conformitie'.[145] The rector of Hanwell considered that the recent suppression of the conventicle at Calthorpe House in Banbury would add weight to his arguments about the dangers of schism. These Oxfordshire incumbents were voicing an opinion which was shared by the majority of their Anglican contemporaries. In the account of his diocese which William Lloyd, Bishop of Peterborough, prepared for Archbishop Sancroft in 1683, he laid great stress on the importance of the work of the magistrates in suppressing conventicles. Within eight months of taking up office, in 1679, Lloyd had accounts of twenty-nine conventicles meeting in Northamptonshire. The justices, encouraged by the reaction to the Rye House Plot, which had once again identified Protestant dissent with sedition, began in earnest to

---

[140] See below, p. 14.
[141] See below, p. 14.
[142] See below, p. 20.
[143] See below, p. 22.
[144] See below, pp. xxxix–xl.
[145] See below, p. 14.

enforce all the penal laws against nonconformity. 'They have succeeded so well in that work', wrote Lloyd, 'as to convince the boldest obstinate Phanaticks that the laws and government are too hard for their schism'. The result of their care and vigilance was that, by 1683, there were no longer any notorious conventicles meeting in public in the diocese. This, together with the efforts of the parochial clergy in convincing the individual dissenters of the error of their ways, had reduced the number of non-communicants from 2200 to 100.[146]

The letters of the incumbents of Adderbury, Hethe, Ibstone, and Aston Rowant illustrate the importance in combating dissent of the help, not only of the magistrates, but also of the influential men in the parishes and of the parish officials. In Bray Doyly, the Quakers of Adderbury, indeed of north Oxfordshire, had a leader of considerable social standing in the county. As lord of one part of the manor, he could provide tenancies for Quakers. The inclusion of £1100 of debts owing to him among his assets at his death, suggests that he used much of his means to give direct financial aid to his fellows.[147] His influence made it impossible for the curate of Adderbury to reduce the number of dissenters.[148] In Hethe, the influence of the Papist family, the Fermors of Tusmore, as lords of the manor, encouraged the spread of Roman Catholicism.[149] The incumbent of Ibstone found it very difficult to persuade his parishioners to attend church regularly, when the family of the lord of the manor, Sir Henry Allnutt, set a poor example.[150] In Aston Rowant, the vicar had problems with his parish officials, which were made worse by the support they received from the lord of the manor, John Clerke. Clerke had refused, ever since the end of the civil war, to give the incumbent a customary amount of wood each year.[151] Reynolds wrote twice to Fell after his visitation, first in June, giving an account of his struggle to prevent the election of a churchwarden who was sympathetic to the dissenters. Mr Clerke had been persuaded to nominate a John Monday, who, having recently married the daughter of the principal Anabaptist in the parish, could probably have been relied on not to present the dissenters at the archdeacon's and bishop's visitations. It was only with difficulty that the vicar had been able to exercise his right to choose as churchwarden a man who was a regular attender at church and a communicant. In his second letter, at the beginning of July, Reynolds reported that the dissenters had so far been protected from prosecution at

---

[146] MS. Rawl. D. 1163, especially ff. 12, 20.
[147] MS. Wills Oxon. 19/1/4, Sept. 1696.
[148] See below, p. 1.
[149] See below, p. 21.
[150] See below, p. 22.
[151] *V.C.H., Oxon.*, VIII, 36.

the Quarter Sessions, because the parish constable (a man whom Fell had removed from the post of churchwarden because he refused to receive communion) had made false presentments to the justices.[152] Two other incumbents emphasized in their letters the importance of the churchwarden's role. John Bushell had upset most of his parishioners in Lewknor, by choosing 'a serviceable churchwarden, who proves as impartial and inexorable as death . . . and is not discourag'd from his duty by any of their frownes, obloquies or threats'.[153] At Enstone, the vicar had discovered that a pamphlet was in circulation which produced arguments from the Scriptures to show that churchwardens should not present dissenters.[154] Fell asked Archdeacon Halton to procure a copy of this, but there is no record of his having been able to do so.[155]

Altogether thirteen of the Oxfordshire incumbents who wrote to Fell expressed the opinion that the civil power must be used in the attempt to enforce conformity. Thomas Thomlinson and John Kerie both thought that it was only fear of punishment that made many of their parishioners conform.[156] Richard Evans, John Bushell, and George Vernon all believed that a strict application of the penal laws, especially the 12*d*. fine for each Sunday that anyone was absent from his parish church, would make people 'perfectly conformable to the church and its laws, or at least as far as we can judg by their outward actions'.[157] George Vernon, who was rector of Bourton on the Water and of St John and St Michael in Gloucester, as well as of Sarsden, expressed similar views in print, when he became involved in a controversy with Sir Thomas Overbury the younger, a neighbour of his in Gloucestershire. His object in publishing *Ataxiae Ostaculum* in 1677 was 'to remove false pretences of conscience in matters of religion, and to defend the magistrate's power in the same'. The dissenter's appeal to his own conscience as his ultimate guide in religion was exasperating to those who believed and taught that salvation lay in acceptance of the doctrine and liturgy of the established church.[158] Vernon thought 'queries and scruples in matters of religion . . . certain signes of a weak and childish, or of a cavilling and froward judgment'. The penal laws should be enforced against the persistent dissenter, in

---

[152] See below, pp. 4–5.
[153] See below, p. 26.
[154] See below, p. 16.
[155] See below, p. 34.
[156] See below, pp. 30, 13.
[157] See below, pp. 21, 26, 29.
[158] The contrast between the Quakers at Black Bourton, who 'held that the rule of their conscience is Christ the liveing word, who by his holy spirit immediately leads them into all trueth, without the ministry of a dead letter', and the rector of Salford, who was happy to obey, 'for then I have the wisdome of my superiour either for my warrant, or my excuse', is most marked; see below, pp. 6, 28.

order to save his soul, and also because, in disobeying the laws of the church, he was endangering the peace of the state — 'for the interest of both those societies are so twisted and united, that like Hippocrates's twins, they laugh and weep, live and dye, both together'. The relationship between church and state was the chief justification of the use of the civil power against religious offenders. To Anglicans and Royalists, the principal lesson of the civil war — that dissent from the established church led to attempts to overthrow the established government — had been reinforced by the involvement of some dissenters, first in Venner's conspiracy, then in the Rye House Plot. Vernon concluded his argument, in a phrase which echoed countless upholders of the established church and monarchy, that not to use the powers given to the magistrates was to 'encourage men in their schisms and separations, disobedience and rebellions'.

The fear that conventicles were power-houses of rebellion proved empty. From very early on, the Quakers had been opposed to the use of force in pursuit of any aim, secular or religious. What they, like the Anabaptists and the Independents, sought from the civil power in the 1660s was toleration, the right to worship God as they thought fit, outside the framework of the established church. The Presbyterians also came round to this view, during the 1670s and 1680s, as their hopes of altering the structure of the established church, so that they could be included in it, gradually faded. Only when the pro-Catholic policies of James II drove them to it, did the majority of Anglicans come to see the virtues, even the necessity, of such a toleration.

The surviving letters of incumbents in 1682, with Fell's queries and Archdeacon Halton's replies, show that many of the conventicles reported in 1669 continued to thrive into the 1680s. In the north of the diocese, conventicles at Adderbury, Bloxham, Deddington, and Banbury alarmed incumbents of these or neighbouring parishes.[159] Similarly in the west, conventicles at Bampton, Leafield, Chipping Norton, Burford, Witney, Charlbury, and Hook Norton caused concern to parochial clergy and diocesan officials,[160] while in the south only Aston Rowant, Lewknor, Warborough, and Henley worried the authorities.[161] Most of these towns still had nonconformist meeting places in 1738, when the replies of incumbents to Bishop Secker's visitation inquiries provide the next survey of dissent in the diocese.[162] From this it can be seen that the action taken by Fell, his archdeacon and incumbents, did not suppress the conventicles,

---

[159] See below, pp. 1, 6, 14, 18.
[160] See below, pp. 5, 10, 33, 34.
[161] See below, pp. 4, 7, 26, 34.
[162] Printed, O.R.S., xxxviii (1957). For details of dissent in these towns, see the notes below.

though it may well have reduced the number of individual dissenters. It is noticcablc that two of the largest conventicles reported in 1669 — in the market towns of Thame and Henley — were still flourishing in 1738, as were those in Oxford, Bicester, Banbury, Chalgrove, Witney, and Hook Norton; a fact which supports the thesis that dissent took firmer root in the towns than in the rural areas, where people were more dependent on Anglican landlords.[163] Most of the conventicles which existed between 1676 and 1686 survived to enjoy the toleration accorded to them after the Revolution of 1688.[164] In 1738, almost all the Anglican clergymen who commented on the numbers of the dissenters in their parishes, were convinced that they were decreasing. Of more concern to most of them, as it had been to the incumbents of Caversham, Hanwell, and Ibstone in 1682, was the increase in the number of 'neglecters'.

The vicar of Bladon summed up the situation in 1738, when he reported that the decline in the number of Presbyterians and Independents in Woodstock was 'not to be imputed by any extraordinary increase of knowledge; or regard to unity, order, etc., but to that general decline of zeal and inclination to divine things in any shape, by which most men are now-a-days become but too indifferent to religion in ev'ry shape. Hence also there are, in all places, more absentees than dissenters'.[165] The problems of the spiritual decline of the early eighteenth century were to affect established church and nonconformists alike.

---

[163] See M. R. Watts, *The Dissenters* (Oxford, 1978), p. 286.
[164] Only those at Aston Rowant and Heyford were recorded as coming to an end during Fell's episcopate, see below, p. 36.
[165] *Secker Visitation*, p. 18.

I
LETTERS TO FELL FROM OXFORDSHIRE INCUMBENTS, 1682

[MSS. Oxf. Dioc. c.430, ff. 1–36, c.650, f. 27. The headings have been added by the editor.]

f.1   ADDERBURY

My Lord,
    I am exceedingly troubled that my manyfold affaires besides some bodily indisposition, has hindered me from so timely and just obedience to your Lordship's commands as I ought. I am sure nothing in the world shall ever be more welcome to me, and I hope I may be yet so fortunate as to give you better assurance of it.
    Concerning the state of the Parish in which I have this 3 yeares officiated (and a very large Parish it is) I should be very happy and give up my accounts to God and your Lordship with more joy, could I give that satisfaction you may expect, but I doubt I shall not be able. For, besides that indifferency and coldnesse in religion, and that worldly mindednesse, which possesses the generality, wee have a factiouse schismatical spirit which reigns amongst us; wee have two fruitful nurseries unfortunately placed amongst us, one Quakers, the other Presbyterian.
    As for the Quakers I acknowledge my unsuccesfulnesse, notwithstanding my endeavours to win 'em and lessen their numbers, for Bray D'oyly[1] who is the ringleader and Lord of one part of the manour, upon any vacancy in it, fills it with Quakers from other parts, and it seems resolves to admit no Tenents but such. They keep a constant meeting Sundays and Wednsdays in a house built upon his estate for that purpose.[2]
    The Presbyterrians, about a litle mile from the Towne, they keep a Conventicle, peopld from all quarters round about.[3] Mr. Wheately[4] (son of a better man) of Hempton in the Parish of Dadington, and one Mr. Stedham[5] of Banbury, are the preachers there, which conventicle is always the great Exchange for Politics and, by reason of our numerouse freeholders hereabouts, the County Knights are generaly chosen in it.

This has a very ill influence upon all our neighbourhood and more especialy upon this Parish, for tho' wee have very few indeed that wilfully and constantly absent themselves from the offices of the Church, fewer then any place in the County considering our great number of Parishioners, yet they, many of 'em, will stragle one part of the day thither, when they duely attend the public worship of God on the other, and they seem to be like the borderers betwixt two kingdomes one can't well tell what Prince they are subject to. This, my Lord, has been my great trouble but unfortunately living under a slack magistracy has been out of my power to redresse I doe assure your Lordship I have used all Christian endeavours as far as my ability could extend and I doe with some comfortable boldnesse assure you I have lost no ground since I came hither. I shall by the first opportunity I can get pay my duty to your Lordship at Oxon and then give you a more particular account.

In the meane time I humbly beg your Lordship's prayers and blessing and that I may be esteemd my Lord your Lordship's most dutiful and obliged servantt: Robt. Parsons.[6]

Adderbury   June 24th   1682[7]

f.2   ASTON ROWANT

My Lord,
In obedience to your Lordshipp's Charge at the visitation I did acquaint the Dissenters within my Parish of your desire to have an account of theire severall reasons why they did not come to Church: and haveing occasion in the meane time to choose a Churchwarden in the roome of the person your Lordship put out,[8] I thought it convenient to see how they would behave themselves in that affaire before I went to demand theire answers: and haveing appointed Monday last (being Whitsun-Monday) for the Election to the intent that all that were disposed might receave the Sacrament on Whitsunday and haveing also given notice at the end of Divine Service, of the Election the Next day — when the Neighbours came to meete after Morning Prayer upon the Monday, I found the Dissenters had bin contriveing to play one of theire old Games over againe, and in order thereunto had bin with Mr. Clerke[9] and Prevailed with him to Nominate one John Monday a Smith, a young man newly Married to the Daughter of Richard Chitch the Cheife of the Dissenters and at whose house the Conventicles have bin kept neare this 20 yeares.[10] I saw the Dissenters were all neare at hand to back Mr. Clerks Nomination with theire Votes, so I told him it was strange the last vice-churchwarden should be putt out for not receaveing the Sacrament, and that they should nominate one to succeede who had not received the

Sacrament within a yeare last past, and I did beleive none of them could prove he did ever receave it in his life and seldom came to Church. — I told them it was in vaine to enter into further controversy, only that I had a right, togeather with the rest of my Brethren of the Clergy, when there are two Church-wardens to be chosen in a yeare, to nominate one, and that accordingly I did Nominate Hugh Hunt of Kingston[11] a good farmer who keeps to Church and receaved the sacrament on Whitsunday: and that I left it to your Lordshipp to admitt which you please to be sworne. I hope your Lordship will give effectuall orders that the said Monday do not gett himselfe secretly sworne by the Chancellor or any other meanes, and that the Apparator may have order to warne Hunt to take his Oath. After I came out of the Church the said Chitch the Ring-leading Dissenter came to me and Insolently askt me what my reason was to opose the Parish: I told I did only vindicate my owne right, and that I would never give my vote for any Man to be a Church officer who did not frequent the Church and sacrament. By all this your Lordshipp will guesse they are too much moved, to expect a civil answer from them at present; but your Lordshipp shall have an account of what they have to say for themselves so soone as I can any way obtaine it. Your Lordship will perceive the greate difficulty of breakeing this Dissenting Knott, because of the advice and support Mr. Clerke gives them. However I shall not be wanting to do my utmost, begging only your Lordshipp's Blessing and Assistance in the undertakeing.

Your Lordshipp's Most humble and obedient servant   Tho. Reynolds[12]

Aston   June 8th   1682

f.3   ASTON ROWANT

My Lord,
I herewith send your Lordshipp the plainest answers I can gett from the severall Dissenters and absenters from church, why they do not resort to it — within the parish of Aston Rowant, being of the Anabaptist perswasion.

Richard Chitch[13] (theire Champion) at whose house most of the Conventicles have bin kept in Kingston in the said parish above this 20 yeares — saith that he ownes all the Ordinances of Jesus Christ: but denys there is any such thing as a Church in the sence in which it is taken in the Laws of England (for a publick place or building sett apart for Gods service where those that professe the Name of Christ are obleiged to Assemble to worship God according to Christ's own Institution) for if there be such a Church (he saith) there can be no Martyr.

He also saith he ownes Divine Service, because he is sure if it be Divine it must be of Divine Institution.

William Turner[14] (theire speaker for many yeares) hath bin twice att Church, being afraid not only to answer this question, but of the proceedings of the Civil power: and now he saith he is none of them, but will continue to come to Church.

Christopher Crook[15] though intreated to stay (when he was with me upon businesse) while I might speake a few words with him, which I intended upon this subject, pleaded so much hast that I found him shy to answer this question: upon which I did engage one of his nearest Relations (who keeps fast to the Church, and from whom he expects a Considerable estate), to try if his reasons for absenting could be obtained, and he answers in the Generall, that he cannot come, and sometimes adds some of the old empty reasons, because of the Mixture of good and bad in our congregations and at our ordinances etc.

John Chitch the Elder[15] I cannot yet speake with.

John North junior[16] whose Father hath bin long a stubborne and Resolute seperatist and is still liveing but so weake that he is never likely to go out of doores; and his son haveing a wife and children and expecting a Considerable Estate from his Father saith, it may be he may come to Church if it please God to take his Father, but he is not willing to be under the obligation of a Promise.

Mr. William Stafford a Great Olivarian, and in those dayes an officer: and to this time a great promoter of separateing principles: in church affaires holds that every one that worships God in the Publick place is a Barbarian to him, and he the like to them: upon my first publishing the Question, left the Parish and I have not since heard where he is.

Thomas Bennet Shoomaker, and Practitioner in Physick,[17] saith, there shall be no occasion of complaint against him: and that he will come to Church.

John Chitch junior Maultster[18] (son of the Ringleader Richard Chitch) it is beleived, would come to Church but dares not while his father lives: unlesse by the meanes now used his father be driven unavoidably from his long-continued practise of absenting.

All these except John Chitch the Elder haveing wives, I presume your Lordship will suppose to be of theire husbands' minds: though sometimes against theire wills, and only in outward shew, and I do truly beleive it is so with some of these. But that your Lordship may see we have done what time would give us leave hitherto to reduce all those to church (tho' they have bin, at all the monthly meetings of the Justices since your Lordshipp's visitation, kept off from being questioned by the Civil Magistrate by the false presentments of Richard Cooper[19] whom your Lordshipp put out from being vice-churchwarden, but still retaines the office of Constable). We have (for all this) at length gotten foure of the Principall Dissenters vizt.

Richard Chitch, John Chitch the Elder, Christopher Crooke, and Mr. William Stafford presented upon the Oathes of the Officers for absence from our Parish Church for severall Sundayes past: and att the same time the said Richard Cooper was bound over to the next Quarter Sessions (by the Hohourable Captain Bertie[20] and Mr. Gregory)[21] and to be upon the behavior in the meane while. This being all I have to trouble your Lordship with at present I remaine

Your Lordship's Most Humble and Most Faithfull servant

Tho: Reynolds

Aston Rowant[22]   3rd July   1682.

f.4   BAMPTON

A List[23] of the Names of Schismaticall Dissenters within the Parish of Bamton[24] humbly to bee presented to the Right Reverend Father in God my Lord Bishop of Oxford.

Quakers   1. Bettres not obstinate.[25]   2. Wheeler and his wife and daughter.[26]   3. Windows and his wife.[27]   4. Goody Wats.[28]   5. Widow True.[29]   6. Hill.[30]   7. Wise and his wife.[31]   8. Crips and his wife.[32]   9. William Warwick and his wife.[33]   10. Bartlet's wife of Aston:[34] all desperate.

Anabaptists   1. Carpenter, his wife and children.[35]   2. May.   3. Mrs. Brickland.[36]   4. Wellicom and his wife.[37]   5. Oakes's wife.[38]   6. Evans.[39]   7. Clinch, his son and daughter in law.   8. Williams his Son and Daughter-in-Law.   9. Coles's wife.   10. Harris and his wife.   11.   Pears and his wife. blinde and incorrigibl.

Heathens   1. Hill.   2. Feild.[40]   3. Skinner.[40]   4. Goody Green.   5. Sidwell[40] who owns conviction and promises amendment. The Rest except Feild who is a licentious villain, ar in their Moralls irreproachabl but never mingl with any religious assembly.

Papists   Two, Winterburn[41] and Farmer, impenetrabl to the truth.

f.5   BLACK BOURTON

My Lord,
There are but two profess'd Sectaries (which are both Quakers) belonging to our Parish, one of them is an old passionate man, called John Turner,[42] who (being our Herdsman) lives in a house on the common adjacent to Clanfeild, he professes himself to be a rigid Quaker, but his

neighbors say, he never frequents any meetings himself, but only his wife, who (being poore) are supposed to receive contribution from the brethren; their reason of separateing from the church (they say) the King knows already, but upon further urgency, they alledge conscience for it, yet deny the holy scriptures to be either the rule theirof, or of judging spirits by, whether they be of God, pretending that the rule of their conscience is Christ the liveing word, who by his holy spirit immediately leads them into all trueth, without the ministry of a dead letter. Their further allegations were so absurd and contradictory (tho not in their own eyes, yet) to any men, but of ordinary common sense, that I think them much unworthy your Lordship's cognisance.

The other Quaker is a single man, of a middle age, called John Monke,[43] a Wheele-wright by trade, whose father is a Quaker liveing at a towne called Filkins, where the said John Monke his son has lain sick for some time, he was expected at oure towne about a fortnight since, but they say he is relapsed, wherefore his comeing being uncertaine makes me unwilling to expect him any longer than this visitation, humbly begging your Lordship's pardon for my silence thus long.

Your Lordship's most humbly devoted servant   Jer. Bates[44]

Blackbourton.[45]   September the 20th. 1682.

f.6   BLOXHAM

My Lord,

Since I was last to wait upon your Lordship I have used my utmost endeavours to reduce some refractory persons to their due obedience, and that not without some hopes of success, some having already publickly engaged to come to the Church, that have absented themselves for many years past. But I find the greatest part of the Quakers and Anabaptists so ignorant and obstinate, that 'tis in vain to offer any thing to their consideration: this my Lord Bishop of Landaff,[46] Mr. Parsons[47] and others know by experience as well as I. Besides, to my knowledge the ringleaders of the several sects are so mightily enraged of late (since their designe, I hope, is like to miscarry), that 'tis their business in all places bitterly to inveigh against the Church of England and the Episcopal Clergy giving them the most invidious Character they can invent, perswading their ignorant followers to believe (as they are too credulous in that Case) that they are almost at St. Peters Palace already, and there are many pestilent books privately printed and carefully spread abroad to that end and purpose. Your Lordship may with Confidence believe that I am firm to the Interest of the Church, and that I shall endeavour in all things to approve my selfe,

My Lord, Your Lordship's most obedient faithful servant and curate Nic: Page[48]

Bloxham.[49]   June 9. —82.

f.7   CHALGROVE

Right Reverend

In obedience to your Lordship's commands at Henly, these are humbly to informe your Lordship, that there is an Chalgrave[50] but one that dissents from the church of England, and that one a Roman Catholick; which person I have through my endeavours reclaimed, and brought to a compleat conformity to the prasent establish'd lawes. But in the chappelry of Berwick Salome, belonging to the mother church of Chalgrave, there are three dissenters; one whereof is Joseph Wise,[51] who holds the Jewish sabbath, and is against infant baptisme, being of one Stannett's[52] church, living in Wallingford castle. Another is John Low, an Independent, of Covin's church of Warborough.[53] The third is Thomas Binham[54] a Quaker, whose certaine meeting place I cannot as yet learne. I have had severall conferences with these persons, and have with the utmost of my power and ability endeavoured to reduce them to the church, but with no successe, for they appear to me unalterably fix'd to their respective perswasions, which since I cannot help, I rest satisfy'd in doing my duty wherein I shall acquit my self,

My Lord, your Lordship's in all filial obedience most humble servant Ri: Manning[55]

June 10 (82)

f.8   CAVERSHAM

May it please Your Lordship,

In obedience to your Lordship's commands, I gave the parishioners notice in the Church upon Sunday after Ascension day, that on White Sunday following I should administer the holy Sacrament, and to stir them up to their duty, I did read the second exhortation, as is appointed in case of the peoples negligence. I also inform'd them, that I had a strict charge from Your Lordship to send an account of all persons, who did not receive the Communion at Easter, and neglected to do it on Whitsunday. My Lord, I administer'd the Sacrament three Sundaies successively at Easter, (which is once more than usuall of late) on purpose to give oportunity to all that were willing, and to allow no pretence of excuse for others; and, by what I am inform'd had more Communicants than hath been of late years. However, these persons following are none of that number,[56] vizt.

Mrs. Blunt[57] & her son
Mr. Charles Blunt[58] } Papists

Mr. Robert De La Vall[59]
Edward Berrey, constable[60] } suspected to be so but come to Church tho seldom

Captain Thomas Curtice[61]
Richard Soundy[61] } Quakers

The Earle of Kildares servant,[62]
a French man
Roger Forster
John Justice[63]
Robert Percey
John Pace, senior
John Pace, junior } Dissenters and never came to Church (except once or at most twice) these twelve months.

Mr. Thomas Brigham
Mr. Anthony Brigham
John Percey[63]
Athanasius Snadhams
Christopher Hall
Richard Dean } These come very seldom in a morning but never in an afternoon.

Mr. Richard Blackhall
Mr. Giles Gregory[64]
John Stephens
William Curtice
Thomas Phillips
William Hill
William Lovejoy
Mr. Thomas Cartwright } These come very constantly in a morning, but seldom in the afternoon.

Leonard Cole, senior
Leonard Cole, junior
Thomas Castle
Michael Hamblen } These come to Church oftener in the afternoon than the morning.

Thomas Simmons, Churchwarden the last year
Thomas Wicks, present Churchwarden
John Fruen, overseer of the poor
Henry Binfield
Edward Fruen
Thomas Stevens
William Stevens
Nicholas Salter
John Butler
Henry Lovejoy
Edward Collis
William Willier

These frequent the Church both morning and afternoon nor do I hear that any in the parish (except those marked out on the other side) do go to Conventicles.

At Easter and Whitsunday above an hundred persons received; and at Christmasse about twenty.

I administer the Sacraments thrice at Easter, once at Whitsunday, once at Michaelmas and once at Christmas.

f.9

This my Lord is the exactest account my memory can dictate, for I did not take a particular Catalogue of those persons who received at Easter, but I do not in the least dout that any of these did; tho' most of them (except the Dissenters) will I hope receive the communion at another time. I was two whole daies in going about the parish to Dissenters and Recusants, (some of which live four mile from the Church)[65] but they either denyed themselves or were not at home, only John Justice; with whom I convers'd above an hour. He seem'd a little satisfyd with my discourse and I hope in time it will have effect upon him: for since, both Roger Forster and he have been at Church at a funerall sermon on Munday was sevennight: they were uncovered at prayers, but put their hatts on at Sermon time. My Lord, I humbly beg your Lordship's pardon that I sent not this account sooner: but I was desirous to send Your Lordship word also how it is resented which in briefe is thus: The Parish are much displeased with me about it, thinking it the effect of my too forward zeal, rather than the obligation of Your Lordship's commands, or my duty. Many are their arguments, too tedious and simple for Your Lordship's knowledge: the mainest is, that my Predecessor never concern'd himself in it: to which my common answer is, that either he had not the same injunctions given him by Your Lordship, or a better way to satisfy his Conscience in disobeying them than I have as yet found out. My Lord as I publickly inform'd the parish, that neither fear, interest nor affection should move me to be partiall; so malice or revenge hath not the least influence upon me in this account; If it answer Your Lordship's expectations, or testify my desire to fullfill Your Lordship's commands; I hope my willingnes may in some measure expiate my defects in the performance; and I value not the imputations of others, so long as I approve my selfe

My Lord, Your Lordship's Most obedient and most dutyfull servant and Curate   Peter Shelley[66]

Cawsham[67]   June 20, 1682.

f.10   CHARLBURY

Right Reverend Father in God
I have in obedience to your Lordship's command been to visit dissenters. But in regard I have so many towns belonging to my Parish I cannot at present give an account of all. It is a busy time with country people, some I find at home but some I fear will never be found if they can avoid it. The Field town,[68] and Chippingnorton[69] doe us great harm. I hope in a little more time I shal give a more perfect account of all, I am

your Lordship's most dutiful son and obedient servant   Will. Coles[70]

Charlbury[71] — August 1st

f.11

Dissenters in Charlbury

Alexander Harris and his wife[72]
Thomas Busby his wife and daughter[73]
Henry Shod.[74] James Tustle   } Quakers
Goodman Strength and his wife[75]
Goodman Scudder and his wife[76]

Richard Clare[77]
Richard Carpenter[77]   } Independents
Timothy Parish[78]

Goodwife Miles[79]   } Papists
Goodwife White[80]

Chilson

Mistress Hawze
John Harris and wife[81]
Thomas Grant and his wife[81]   } Independents
Widow Titmars
Richard Brooks and his wife and son[81]   Quakers

Shorthampton

Mr. Harris[82]   I cannot tell what

Chadlington Fawler and Finstock[83]

I intend to visit again

f.12   CHASTLETON

Right Reverend Father,
 It is the joy of my heart that I can assure your Lordship that at present there is neither Papist nor any kind of Dissenter whatsoever within my Parish. And I shall thro' Gods Blessing and the constant encouragement which your Lordship gives by your owne Exemplary Piety and Prudence, use my uttmost diligence and endeavour that it may continue soe. And that both for the wellfare of the peoples soules, and for the comfort of him who is
 your truely Obedient and Dutifull Son, John Holloway[84]

Chastleton.[85]   June 6th   1682.

f.13   CHINNOR

My Good Lord,
 According to your Lordshipp's commands I have conferred with Richard Gom and his wife[86] both Quakers and the onely Dissenters in my Parish. After many words, and the most reasonable perswasions to conformity the Answer they returne is this — That they know noe reason why they should bee forced to appeare at Worship, which theyre Consciences cannot approve of as spirituall, and agreeing with the light. And that they were ready to suffer but in noe wise to conforme.
 Bishopp Paul[87] (when Rector heere) had frequent discourses with this woman, but could never in the least prevayle with her. And lately by the order of the Justices they have suffered severall distresses on theyre goods, soe stiffe and stubborne are the poore creatures in theyre errours. All which I leave to your Lordshipp's consideration and Remayne
 Your Lordshipp's most obedient servant   Steph. Jay[88]

Chinner.[89]   June 6th   1682.

f.14   CLANFIELD

My Lord,
 You injoynd us to go particularly to each dissenter . . .[90] reason why

they came not to church, and return those . . .⁹⁰ their names your Lordship had given in the last visitation and therf[ore] I presume it wil not be expected here.

The first I demanded a reason from professes himself a Papist, he told me it was the good nature of the Papists and the il nature of Protestants that wrought upon him.

I askt a Quaker why he would not come to church. I'le tel thee, sais he, why I can't come to thy church. I have set my hand to the plough and I can't look back. Another told me the Church of England has err'd from the truth that is in Christ Jesus therfore they had separated themselvs, as a holy and pure people, as Enotch, Enotch (for so he notcht the word) was a perfect man and walk't with God, with a deal of canting rabble, the pride and insolence of these filthy dreamers is intolerable. The Papist has promist hee'l come again to church, for the other I fear there's no reducing them, it were wel if they seduced not others.

There is a widow with us has renounced the assembly ever since her husband died, it seems she swoons if she comes near the place where her husband was buried.

Some are hard of hearing among us, some want clothes, both, hearts. Twere happy if these evils could be redrest, I shal not be wanting to what lies in my power. I must not deny that your pious exhortation left some deep sentiments on my spirit, while you spoke with that Authority that was meet and that candor and clemency that was obliging. My Lord, if you have further to command me I shal endeavor to perform it as is becoming

Your Lordship's most faithful and obedient servant   Edw. Tyrer⁹¹

From Clanfield⁹²   August 22, 1682.

f.15   COMBE AND STONESFIELD

To the Reverend Father in God John Lord Bishop of Oxford.

In obedience to your Lordship's command (I Thomas Ashfield,⁹³ Rector of Long Coome and Stunsfield⁹⁴ in this county of Oxford) have discoursed with severall of the Decenters for not coming to Church, where George Weston⁹⁵ the capitall and chief Quacker answers me that if our Church were the true Church, and wee the true ministers of the Gospell he would come and heare us, but since it is not soe, the Scripture commands them to with-drawe. The names of the other are Robert Weston,⁹⁵ brother to the said George, with Mary the wife of Richard Ganner, and Marg. Rowell, Elizabeth the wife of James Weston, Elizabeth the wife of Richard Morris and Alice Laughton answered that they would give theire answere themselves, and if your Lordshipe please to send for them.⁹⁶ Alice Hurst of Long Coome⁹⁷ answered me that she had made choice of the Romish religion, and did intend to live and die in the same. These are all the Decenters in the Towns above mencioned to the best of my knowledge. Tho. Ashfield.

[The following letter appears in MS. Oxf. Dioc. c.650, f. 27][98]

Cornwell

Reverend Father in God
John Kerie in the dec. of Chipping-Norton humbly lays before you these greivances. 1 The Churchway is quite walled up by Sir Faire-Meddow Penyston. A way set out within the compass of 20 yeares by a decree in Chancerie & the foure witnesses alive at this present day, so that there is no excuse to be made for it, no custom to be pleaded nor law to defend it, only peremtorie resolution. So that the Parishoners cannot possibly come to church unless they trespass throw my whole yard every such time, 2 cottages only excepted. 2ly The same person hath totally deprived me of the water belonging to my house, without which there is no subsistance & 3ly The mounds of the churchyard are utterly decayed, & Sir Fa. Pe. hath all at his command, & he refuseth to repair them. 4ly Our bell is removed into such a place that it is impossible unless the wind sit in the east for any of the inhabitants to heare it, but the Clerke. 5ly We have no sort of dissenter in our Parish at present, but it is to be feared this will force them to become such, if great ceare be not taken to prevent it. Men being naturally inclined to eas, & the fear of punishment more than love of God makes many in this juncture of time appeare in our assemblies
Yours   John Kerie[99]   Rector de Corn[well][100]

Aprill the: 25. 82

f.16 Deddington

My Lord,
According to your order at your vissitation I have been with the dissenters in my parish to know their reasons why they do not come to church. Mr. Whately[101] a nonconformist minister told me that he had severall reasons but he did not think it fit to declare them. I askt him why? and he told me becaus he did not expect any sattisfaction. I told him if I was not able to sattify him your lordship would send some person from Oxford, but that did not pleas him, yet he was at church after the prayers were over last Sunday morning. The next my Lord is one Philip Ordoway[102]

his reason that he told me was this, God commands him to worship him in spirit and truth and that he could not in our publick worship becaus we use set forms of prayers, no arguments that I could use would perswade him to the contrary. A third and fourth persons are one John Bignell and his wife.[103] When I told them that your Lordship sent me to them, they made me this answer that they did not know what your Lordship or my self had to do to concern our selves with them. I told then it was your Lordship's desire to have them sattisfied. I told them likewise what my own duty was they being under my charge but nothing would prevail. These four persons goe by the names of presbiterians. A second sort my Lord are Annabaptists, their names are these, Thomas Triplet and his wife, Thomas Toms and his wife, John Rews,[104] William Rews and his wife,[105] Francis Winter and his wife, Thomas Makepeace and his wife,[106] some of them would give me no reason at all and they others told me it was against their consciences and they would not come. A third sort are Quakers Katherine Owen[107] the wife of Thomas Owen, Edward Smith and his wife, Anthony Prentice,[108] and a servant of Thomas Owen whose name I cannot tell. These persons insteed of reasoning did nothing but cavill. This is my lord the account of my parish. I gave the sacrament my Lord according to your command when I was last to wait upon your Lordship, and we were but nine in all. Mr. Whately our schoolmaster[109] went from home before the time came. This is all at present that I have to acquaint your Lordship with, desireing your Lordship's prayers. I rest my Lord your dutifull and obedient son and servant   Jeremiah Wheate.[110]

Dadington[111]   June the 5. 1682.

f.17   DRAYTON

Mr Ashwell,[112]

I would entreate you to present to my Lord this short account of our small Parish viz: two families are sectarists, the one are called Anabaptists, the other Quakers. I have discoursed with them and altho they can say little, or nothing for their opinions, yet they are willfull. Wee are not like to be long troubled with them. For Gilkes the Anabaptist hath an incurable disease which will shortly put an end to his life, and Millers[113] the Quaker for not paying his Landlord's rent is to hold his farme but one yeare more. They are both very poore as most of the towne besides are. About 4 weomen and one man doe commonly come to our church in the morning and goe to the Conventicle in Banbury in the afternoon.[114] Unles the Conventicles (which are the seminaries of sedition and rebellion) be suppressed, I feare the people will never be brought to any good conformitie. I pray you to present my humble duty and service to my Lord,

and my heartie thankes to his Lordship for his kinde remembrance of me. So wishing you a good journey, I rest
　Your much obliged neighbor　Ad. Morton[115]

Drayton[116]　May 27, '82

f.18　　　　　　　　　　DUNS TEW

　　　　　　　　　　　　　　　　Duns Tew.[117]　July 28, '82
My Lord
　In obedience to your Lordship's Commands, this gives your Lordship Information concerning the Dissenters of this Parish, and my Conference with them. They are but three in number, all Anabaptists and Excommunicated above these twelve moneths for not appearing at Court, upon Summons, after they had been presented by the Churchwardens, but yet they have been alwaies quiet, not endeavouring to pervert any to their Party; nor inviting meetings to the Parish; nor so much as discouraging others of their Families from coming to Church, so far as ever I could understand. With one of them (whom specially I take to be a welmeaning man, his name Abraham Dawes)[118] I confer'd several times formerly untill (I know not for what secret reason) he pray'd me to Forbear. I attempted to do the like with one of the other, but could not be received; whose Refusal together with the Discharge of the first was the cause I did not offer to conferr with the Third being wife to the Second (one Jonas Smalbone)[118] and from whom I had reason to fear a worse reception then from either of the other. Notwithstanding, in obedience to your Lordship I have of late conferr'd with all three, pressing upon them the Sinfulness of Separation, vindicating our Church and endeavouring to remove their Scruples and refell their opinions; and that not only with a more fair hearing then I could expect, considering what I had found before, but such as has given me no small hopes of gaining them all before I have done. For I do not think my self discharg'd of the Command laid upon me by your Lordship (as neither of the obligation from God himself) by what I have done already in the present business and this Account of it; but that I stand obliged still to continue my endeavours therein to the uttermost of what is possible for me to do; and so I resolve to do by the grace of God. And this I take to be a great incouragement that I find what I have done already has very much abated their Prejudice, and changed them into a more charitable opinion of our Church, Conformity and Conformists, which is well worth my pains though nothing else be effected. In the prosecution of this and all the other parts of my duty I make bold humbly to crave the assistance of Your Lordship's prayers who am (My Lord)
　Your Lordship's most dutiful servant . Nath. Collier[119]

Answerd[120]

f.19 ENSTONE

Enstone[121]   July the 4th. 1682

My Lord,

Had I not bene deceived, by false promises, of some of my recusants, of a peaceable return to our Church, which if it co'd have bene obteined, wo'd have bene (I conceive) most acceptable, had I not fedd myselfe with these vaine hopes, for so they now prove, this account had longe since come to your Lordship's hande.

I come now (tho' late first) to give your Lordshipp the tru state of my parish, which, tho' not altogether free from fanaticisme, yet I am confident, is as little infected with that spreadeinge contagion, as any parish, of the like extent, within five miles round about us. In our two townes of Enston, wee have only 3 women dissenters who frequent Conventicles, their husbands and familyes comeinge duly to church, beside there is one whole familie, in a hamlet call'd Radford 2 miles distant from our Church, and these make up the total summ. The names of these persons are Mary Righton,[122] the wife of Robert Righton, a substantial Farmer, Elizabeth Read, the wife of William Read, one that showes the water-workes,[123] Ann Allen the wife of Samuel Allen a Farmer, Mr. Edward Busby,[124] his wife and children, a Copieholder of about £40 per Annum. Thes persons I have treated with all meekness, humbly desireinge them to let mee knowe what they had to object against the Church of England from whose Communion they are departed, and findeinge nothinge of moment, they have to say for themselves, save that they stand well affected to their owne way, and their owne leaders, I pressed them with the duty that lyes on them, and all good Christians of preserveinge the peace of the Church, there beinge no one doctrine more earnestly recommended to us by Christ and his Apostles then that, which they by formeinge themselves into seperat Congregations do wilfully violat, a greater sin, than they are aware of. I have further urged them with the scandal they hereby give, not only to our Church at home; but to all other the reformed Churches abroad, which have received our Articles into the harmonie of their Confessions. I have minded them of the advantage they give to the common enemie, who rejoyceth in nothinge more than our divisions, of which they by their emissaries, have bene the original promoters, The fruit of which weake endeavours of mine I finde to bee only this: promises by one or two, of a returne, but hitherto no performance. This obstinacy, I am apt to believe, may in parte bee occasioned by a printed paper,[125] which I am told by one of our late Churchwardens, Mr. Busby aforenamed, hath gott into his hands, and hee further tells mee, the drift thereof is to dissuade Churchwardens from makeinge their presentments, and that the arguments therein conteined, are back'd with scriptures wrested to so vile an use, an artifice, no doubt used by their Leaders, to keep up their faction, so that I feare, it will bee a hard taske, to bringe home the seduced, unless their seducers bee first suppressed, pardon good my Lord, my boldness, in giveinge you my sence, in a matter more fitt for sounder judgments.

I conclude with an humble request to your Lordship, that you will believe mee, a true sonn of the Church of England, and I do hereby promise, that accordeinge to my pore abilityes, I shall in all things obey your Lordship's just commands, and therefore I subscribe myselfe

Your obedient sonn, and most humble servant   John Beckingham.[126]

f.20   FRINGFORD

Most Reverend and much Honoured Lord,

Being disabled by God, to whose Holy will I desire to submit, I could not be present to heare your Lordship charge to the ministers at your visitation in Bissiter. But not long-after by some Charitable brethen that came to visit me I heard it was your Lordship will that we should goe to the Dissenters in our Parishes that withdraw themselves from our Communion and discourse with them about their Schism and Separation. In obedience to your Lordship command I have (as oft heretofore) so lately discoursed with them. But I must with sorrow profess that I have not that perswasive faculty as almost to perswade them to renounce their seperation and come and joyne with us in the worship of God. But God can. Therefore God forbid I should cease to pray for them and all Separatists that their eyes may be opened to see the mischiefs of Separation that they may repent and returne to the fellowship of our Church, that so the Glory of the Primitive Christians may dwell in our land, that as they so wee may be all of one heart and of one soule and there may be no Seperation amongst us, and thereby the designes and hopes of our fiery Enemies by our divisions not onely to Reproach but to destroy us and our Religion may be defeated. And may it be the Glory of our church to be called a Healer of Breaches. I doubt not but there are many Fatherly Abrahams amongst us who would condescend a little in the smallest matters for the sake of saveing Unity, and I hope there are not few Lots amongst them who by charitable condescentions would be won to hearken to Councells of Necessary Union. For the Canaanits are multiplyed in our land. The God of Unity give us all one Heart and way that after the way our bloody enemies call Pestilent Heresie, we may without feare feare the God of our Fathers for ever in England, Amen. So craving your Lordship Pardon, Acceptance and Blessing, I rest, your Lordship's obsequious son and servant   John Bayly.[127]

Fringford[128]   July 13. 82

The names of our dissenters are Robin Statsfield[129] a profest Quaker. He is from home at London. John Payne[130] an old Anabaptist and Excom. I feare resolved in his way. A poore man Robin Savadge[131] a Reputed Papist but will not owne himselfe one to me but rather seemes to disowne it. I prest him much to tell me why he left our Communion but he told me againe and ag[ai]ne he would not then tell me. At p[   ][132] he desired to come again to[   ][132]

f.21 HANWELL

Right Reverend Father in God and my very good Lord,

    In obedience to your Lordship's commands, I have lately made a visitation of my parish, and discoursed with the severall families therof, and more especially with those (according as your Lordship gave mee in charge) whom I thought schismatically affected. I also delivered to some of them that Discourse of St. Cyprian concerning the Unity of the Church which your Lordship caused to be translated into English, and then sent hither (as to other parishes of your Diocess) to be communicated unto them.[133] Some other Bookes also I added therto, the Reading wherof I thought might conduce to the same good End by working in them a good opinion of the publick service of the Church, and shewing them the Necessity of continuing in her Communion and submitting to her orders, together with the great Danger, or rather the utter Destructiveness of Separation. Now what will be the Effect, either of my Discourses, or the reading of the Bookes, which I gave them to peruse, God only knowes, who only can make them effectuall to that end. But though all have not yet given mee that encouragement to hope, which I could have wished yet I hope the best of the major part; and the rather, because I am informed that the factious Conventicle at Cauthrop House in Banbury,[134] (which drew away some of my parishioners, as well as many others in the country round about) hath bene lately forbidden by our Justices, and that therupon none have met there of late. Which prohibition, if it be obeyed for the future, will, I hope, not a little availe towards the reducing of schismaticks, as well in other neighbour Parishes, as mine owne. Neither intend I to stop heer, but as opportunity serves, shall not faile, God willing, for the time to come, either to send for or to visite at their owne Homes, All such under my Charge, whom I judge, in a more particular manner, to need my personall conference in private, namely, the sick and weak, the sad and distressed, who lie under the sore Burden of any Affliction or Temptation, the poor and needy, those who are at difference, the scandalous and extravagant, the grosse Neglecters of Religious Duties, the slanderers and injurers of their neighbours, the ignorant and seduced, with the seducers of others either by their misperswasions, or ill examples. This, I thanke God, I have already, in some measure, by his gracious Assistance, taken some care to doe, neither shall I, I trust in his Grace, neglect it hereafter. And the rather, because I conceive, that I have done more Good among them by my Discourses and Admonitions in private, than by my preaching in publick; though I have not neglected that neither, twise every Lord's Day, my Discourse in the afternoon being commonly a catechisticall lecture on some part of the Catechisme, or our Saviour's Sermon in the Mount, wherein at present I am imployed. And in the Lent time I constantly catechise the children of my Parish in the Afternoons, and then explain the whole Catechisme by parcels in seven plain Discourses, fitted to the capacity of the meanest, that so none may have any just cause hereafter either to complain of mee, or to excuse themselves, that they wanted instruction in the main grounds of Faith, and by that means are like to perish for want of necessary knowledg. When I came hither first, I found severall persons unbaptized, some wherof were very yong, and others more grown up. But at last I prevailed with the parents of the former to bring them unto Baptisme, and to find them out Godfathers and Godmothers; and for the other, I took paines first to instruct them in the Grounds of Religion, and then acquainted them with the nature and obligation of the Baptismall vow, with the high concernment of that Sacrament, in order to the obtaining of Salvation, before that I admitted them therunto. So that many years are past, since I had any person in my parish remaining unbaptized. Besides, at present, I have never a Quaker in my parish, and but one profest Anabaptist, a single woman, who was dipt, as I am informed, by that infamous Sectary Cop,[135] some years before I came hither. I have discoursed with her severall times to convince her of her errour, and ill condition, but hitherto in vain. Yet I purpose to try once more, when ever I can find a convenient time. There is also one other married woman, who hath stood excommunicated some years for obstinatly refusing to return publick Thanksgiving for her safe delivery. Not long after, I obtained the favour of Bishop Blandford, your Lordship's predecessour, for her Absolution, without any charge of fees upon the confessing of her fault, and craving to be absolved. Notwithstanding shee then refused to come in. I heartily wish that the like indulgent proffer which your Lorship lately made, when I last waited on you at Oxford, may meet with better Success, wherof I purpose to give your Lordship an Account ere long; as of some other particulars too, which I cannot so well doe at present. And thus, my Lord, I have endeavour'd to discharge my Duty, and to answer your Lordship's commands, by giving you a Breviate of the state of my parish, and of my owne Imployment heer, with the success therof. Which if it may be acceptable to your Lordship, till I have the Honour and Happines to wait upon you next at Oxford, you will farther incourage and oblige, my good Lord, your Lordship's most humble, faithfull and already much obliged servant to be commanded, Geo. Ashwell[136]

Hanwell.[137]   June the 22nd. — 82.

f.22   HARPSDEN

Right Reverend Father in God.

To every Title drawne off from the Articles of Inquiry in your Lordship's late Triennial visitation I have made particular returnes, except in that one, recommended vivâ voce to us all. Now as to the Endeavour of reducing Dissenters to Conformity, by all possible perswasion, I have since then, syncerely obey'd the Letter of your Lordship's generall Command, and shall pray to God, that the giving of all Diligence, may obtayne the desired effect of your Evangelical Spirit which hath already wrought a wonder, and procured you many praises, but, by their Default, few Proselytes. Howsoever to God's Honour and our Comfort, your saying and Doing, with such fatherly care, and meeke condescending, hath done great right to yourselfe, and the sacred order, and as some of the party (moved with envy) have sayd to me, that you have done their cause a disadvantage and a mischief, by your comeing among them, and Demonstrating your selfe so great a christian, as to heape coales of fire on their head, and over-come evil with good; God grant, we your spiritual sons may walke in the steps, and follow the example, of our ghostly father, in all possible Imitation. For those few of mine (2 of one family, man and wife;[138] and 3 of another, a mother, son and Daughter) I can and will dayly pray, whether they will or no, as I have told them; but I feare they are unreformable, and fit for no other Remedy, but to be sent to the Hospital of St. Jacomo in Rome, provided for the afflicted with Incurable Diseases. To mention the Inquisition in Spayne, or our owne Bedlam in England (two sort of prisons, which a severe Monke sayd, would cure all kinds of offenders) would be abhorrent to a true christian temper, if any milde method may prevayle; which ought to be heartily wisht, but hardly to be expected. Our Adresses to the father of mercy's must be so much more fervent and Devout, for this is an uncleane spirit that is not to be dispossest, unles it be, by prayer and fasting. If it were possible for the kingdom of heaven to suffer such a kinde of violence, as that these fierce spirits should take it by force, they woud ether be a disturbance to the calmest Region of peace, or make themselves unhappy in the Mansions of happines. Your goodnes cannot thinke so ill, that any humane nature should be so much Degenerated, and sunke below it selfe; Nor I my good Lord, had not God, by makeing me your Curate, taught me by wofull Experience (a severe schoole mistresse) who hath made me, to pay deare, for this base learning. If you have charity enough to chide me for the want of it, and withal to pardon the Length of this Impertinency, I shall humbly beg your paternal Benediction, and ever remayne, My Lord, yours in all canonical obedience, Hu. Boham.[139]

Harpesden[140]
June 2 at 3 in the morning.

f.23 HETHE

Right Reverend Father in God, and my honoured Lord, after my most humble service presented etc.

According unto the precept, which your Lordshippe gave unto the whole clergie, at your Lordship's personall visitation lately at Biciter, and to me in particular, after the sacred solemnity of confirmation then, and there, to give you an account in writing and to send unto you a letter of what dissenters are at present in my parish of Heath by, or before the first day of August next. In answer unto your Lordship's command, I doe here humbly declare. That dissenters of any sect there are none in my parish, except a few who doe goe under the name of Roman Catholicks; and those are certaine poore people, that either now are, or have formerly bin labourers unto Mr. Fermore at Tuesmore house[141] neere adjacent unto the village of the aforesaid Heath, some of whom are already excommunicated. The number of them are about eight or nine. The names of them are Edward Justice and his wife,[142] John Gill and his wife,[143] the wife of Emanuell Newton,[144] John Ward, Anne Smith[145] a poore widdow, Jane the wife of John Dagley,[146] and Mary Harvie a poore widdow also. Some have bin slack-commers to church,[147] that are in my parish, whom I have admonished to come duly thither, to joyne with us in the publick worship of God, who since my admonition have appeared at the church in divine service time, and also seemed to be reverend there then. But (my Lord) if that Statute of 1 Eliz. cap. 2, and 3 Jacobi cap. 4 were put strctly in execution, and a precept sent by authority unto all church wardens to collect the forfeitt therin imposed, then doubtless the people would be more diligent in comming to God's divine service.[148] And I suppose there would soone be fewer dissenters throughout the whole Kingdome of what kind soever. Yet a better course taken (in my weak judgment) to decrease the multiplicity of Dissenters of what sort soever (who are as soe many pricking briars, and grieveing thornes, troubling the church) is to humble our selves under the hand of the almighty by fasting, and prayers that he may be pleased to take this good and great work into his owne divine hand to turne these stuburne revolters hearts to the church againe, and to the pious discipline therof.[149] For unless the Lord God be pleased to doe this for us, men are soe wedded to their dogmaticall humors, tho' never soe erronious, that the clergie may time after time admonish, and perswade in vaine, and find litle, or noe remedy or amendment. Paule may plant, and Apollo may water, but it is God that giveth the encrease. God almighty guide and direct. My Lord I shall not trouble your Lordship at present to read any further only be pleased to give me leave to certify, that I am, and shalbe Your Lordship's dutyfull son in all ecclesiastick obedience, and most humble servant,   Ri. Evans,[150] Rector of Heath[151]

July the 6th 1682.

f.24   IBSTONE

Right Honourable and my very good Lord.

In observance of your Lordship's injunction under canonical obedience, I have, in your Lordship's name, treated with the negligent comers to divine service, that is with near all the parish,[152] for they are all very negligent in coming to church, even upon the Lord's day, some few coming it may be after the lessons are read; others at latter end of prayers or the first service, and others not till the sermon begins or is ready to begin, and all these but few of the whole parish neither, many of them coming once in a month or 6 week it may be. And the answer I can obtain from them is a justification of themselves, with great indignation against me, saying they do not forsake the church, they come somtimes, or they go to other churches, and are not, as they are told, obliged to come to their own parish church more than once a month; and one of them told me that Sir Henry Allnut[153] said so, and I have this reason to believe it, that he did it in justification of his son, a parishoner in Stoken Church then presented for not coming to church there. I have several times desired his assistance, he beeing a spectator of their infrequent coming, but could never obtain it, pretending all the parish was not in Oxfordshier, part beeing in the County of Bucks. Sir Henry himselfe is generally at church, but his lady hath not been there this 13 or 14 years, nor received the Sacrament this 5 or 6 years. Tis true shee is many times in pain, but shee is night and day about her house imployed in worldly business, and I would have come at any time to give her the Sacrament if I had been desired. Before Whitsontide I intimated to Sir Henry what charge your Lordship layed upon me to know their answer concerning not receiving the Sacrament etc. Supposing that word to a wise man would have been sufficient, intending to speak with his Lady, if I found he had not disposed her for it; but he shortly falling ill, and there beeing such distraction in the family, more was not to be done. I finde many of the people have, at the bottom, an ill affection for the prayers and governours of the church, really judging the worship tainted with popery, and so come but a little for fashon; at least they make this their secret pretence; but doubtless are so adicted to the world and their own wills, that they look not on the publique worship as advantagious for them, nor are they concerned for the worship of God, beeing sottishly stupid. Doubtless faire perswasion without somthing to constraine them, will not attain their reformation, for they judge what they are not forced to, left to their liberty. The Rule by which (in the least sense) I am to judge them negligent is humane laws, which require their beeing present the intire day and intire service; and they judge if they be sometimes there on the Lord's day in the fore noon, or now and then, they are not reprovable. And as for holy dayes they come not, no tho they have made themselves redy to attend a Christning or Christmas diner. I have warned and perswaded all I can to ingage them to send their children and servants to catechizing so long as that they may be perfect in it, and then understand it farther by an exposition, but cannot obtain their compeney any longer than lent, they having been used to this exercise only 4 or 5 dayes then. They are not really concerned for Religion, that may do them any good. Most, if not all the elder people are unconfirmed. And tho I have perswaded the younger sort to learn the catechisme before I admit them to the Sacrament, and cause them either to be, or to promise to receive confirmation, yet here are two of these who promised, whose parents would not let them come to be confirmed. And because these cannot be had to catechising afterward, and do not put it in practice, Christianity beeing out of fashon, they loose it again. There is one woman in the parish, which is a papist,[154] and will not by any perswasion be converted. And there is a man and his wife, who keepe the Saturday Sabboth,[154] with these I have discourced also, and their final answer is, that if your Lordship can in words shew them an express command of Christ for keeping the Lord's day, they will then keepe it, otherwise they must obey God rather than men. I have spoken with 5 that received not the Communion, and they pretend they were either from home, or sick, or forced to be with such as were so. Thus I have once more ventured to give a true account of the state and condition of my charge, as I did once before, but nothing to purpose beeing acted concerning them, they have been worse ever since, and most malicious against me for so doing. For I gave Bishop Blanford[155] an account concerning them, and the effect was only a letter sent to Justice Allnut, which he read in the church, and when he had done, said, neighbours you here the contents you may do what you please; and the event was, that I was left naked to their rage and fury, and fraud too, for giving account concerning them; and they have been ever since greater neglectors of the divine service, because they think they do the more displease me. Wherefore I must leave these things to your Lordship's greater wisdom. I read, as sent by your Lordship St. Cyprian's tract,[156] and sent word about the parish I had, such a day, something to communicate to them from their Bishop, very few came more, and of those that did, 5 or 6 went out of the church before I had read halfe of it, which used not to do so; and reported there was only a homily which they understood not; and when I enquired the reason, their excuse was they were not well, or went out with such as were not. Two things there are in which I most humbly begg your Lordship's information. The one concernes the exposition of the Church Catechisme given by your Lordship, for I finde there is not a certain understanding amongst us concerning it. Some are of opinion that you require it to be learnt by the younger people of the parish, who are to render us an account thereof; others, that your Lordship expects only, it should be a rule for our expounding of it. The other request is, whether your Lordship's Court hath power to recover tyths or not, for 'tis suggested here, that it hath not.[157] Could I be sufficiently assured from any other, I would not have troubled your Lordship, for I have one in my parish, who having layd down his ground to grass, and sown it with this new found grass[158] for many years, and fedd it with profitable cattle, yet when they are ready to bring profit to the Church, hath for several years driven them away, saying no tyth is due to the Church.[159] Nay I cannot for 3 years together obtain of him so much as any reconing; and tho he agreed for two lambs 3s, and sheard his sheep in the parish, and the tyth white[160] is unquestionably due, yet can I not obtain them from him, no nor so much as my Easter offerings neither. And when his grass wore away, that he was forced to break up his ground, then, when the ground should returne corne tyths, he became mighty cross and troublesom that he might, at his own price, extort the tyths out of my hands,[161] wherefore, besides other devices, he sent one intimately acquainted with me, at a time when I had not leasure of consideration, to ask to take his tyths; I told him 'twas possible he might, and that if I let them it should be in writing, and when I had time things might be considered in order to a bargain: hereupon he seaseth on all his tyths at the rate of 1s 6d. the Acre, without any farther agreement, and even since the Act against frauds and perjury, and his acknowledgment that there is no bargain, he hath holden them ever since the year 1676, breaking up his ground and taking the profit, without giving me any other consideration that the 1s 6d. the Acre, and without any writing. Trusting and Confiding in your Lordship's great Candour and Goodness, he makes bould with your Lordship to request these things, who remaines

    Your Lordship's obedient curate   Richard Parr[162]

Ibston[163]   June the 10th   1682

f.25   Islip

There are noe dissenters from the Church of England in the parish of

Islip,[164] but all of that parish come orderly to divine service and the sacrament.

Edward Penny[165]   Curat

f.26   KENCOT

Kencot[166]   31th July 1682

My Lord,
According to your Lordship's injunction at your Visitation at Wittney I give this account of the persons within my parish, that there are none in it that dissent from the Church of England or refuse to come to the parochiall church for that reason. But one woman doth not frequent it so often as my other neighbours, one reason thereof I knew before, because she hath small children, which require her husband's or her constant tendance. But her being unfit for it, she keeps the more at home, yet I haveing charg'd her with her long absence, have found that her want of decent apparell to appeare among her neighbours hath beene a greater obstacle than the other,[167] which she being convinc't of to be no rationall plea for the neglect of her duty, hath promised oftner to attend the publick service of God, tho since this promise she hath been absent from church 2 Sundayes. But I hope suddenly to bring her to a sense and performance of her duty. After this satisfaction to your Lordship's commands, I humbly crave your Lordship's benediction, and rest, my Lord,
Your Lordship's most obedient servant,   James Oldisworth.[168]

f.27   LEWKNOR

Lewknor[169]   July 4.   82

May it please your Lordship
This comes humbly to begg pardon, for not having been earlier in giving your Lordship the state of my parish. It was because I was taken ill, before I could severally discourse the Sectaries; and now I have done it, I must say of them, they are an unaccountable people, making conscience wholly (though not suffering it to be inform'd) their refuge. And when closely prest to conformity, flying to answers of this kind, that they will put their trust in the Lord, begg his direction what to do, in what way, and after what manner to serve him, and they are sure he will direct them for the best. A Quaker and his wife who have wasted their estate in propagating that faction, are lately run away for debt. An Anabaptist and his wife, by the expiration of a lease, are likewise lately gone hence. Another Anabaptist and his wife, a Satturday Sabbatarian, have put a Tenant into their concerns, lock'd up their Household Goods in some certaine roomes

which they have made a reservation of, and are gone aside to avoyd the penal Lawes,[170] declaring this to be the persecuted Shire of England, and this place hereabouts by reason of ill neighbours (meaning Sir Henry Alnutt[171] and Mr. Gregory)[172] to be the warmest corner in it. Another Anababtist (of considerable estate) and his wife, by name William and Elizabeth North,[173] keep their station, continuing stiff in their perswasion, and inflexible, but, it's conceiv'd, if strictly prosecuted, will make over all they have to their onely sonn, being a Conformist, and be gone alsoe.[174] My Lord, the Sectaries in this place, though favour'd by great persons on both sides us till of late, yet instead of getting ground (as providence has ordered it) have rather lost. None of them, in all the time I have been here, which is 15 yeares, having proselyted any one of their children to their owne perswasion. The Atheists amongst us (which much outnumber the Sectaries)[175] partly terrifyed by the penal Lawes, and partly ashamed by so many eyes at this juncture upon them, begin to observe the Sabbath. This last Easter, my Lord, perceiving the times to look with a kind aspect towards the Church, I gave my selfe up (for which I have ever since been reflected upon as unneighbourly, unpeaceable and troublesome) to make choice of a serviceable churchwarden,[176] who proves as impartial, and inexorable as death, dealing alike with the Atheists and Sectaries, and is not discourag'd from his duty by any of their frownes, obloquies or threats, as neither will, My Lord, your Lordship's most obsequious and obedient servant,

Jo: Bushell.[177]

f.28   MIDDLETON STONEY

Right Reverend Father in God,

May it please your Lordship. Wheras your Lordship was pleased at your late Visitation held att Bisseter, to declare unto the Clergy of this your Lordship's Diocesse there Assembled, That in order to the Conviction and Conversion of the Recusants and other Dissenters in this your Diocesse, your Lordship's Command and Injunction was, that the Severall Ministers, Parsons and Curatts under your Lordship's Jurisdiction, should have Recourse to the severall Houses or Habitations of such Recusants and Dissenters, and there offer themselves and be ready to Confer and Discourse with the said Recusants and Dissenters concerning those Principles of Religion and Parts of Divine Worship, wherin they Dissent from the Orders of the Church of England by Law established, and to endeavour by whatsoever powerfull Arguments to perswade and reduce them to a Conformity with the said Lawes, and within a sett time to give your Lordship an Account of our Proceedings therin, These may give your Lordship to understand, That in the Town and Parish of

Middleton Stony within your Lordship's Diocesse, in the Deanery of Bisseter, wherof I am Constituted, and wherin I execute the Office of Rector, there are no persons, that I know of, inhabitants within the said Parish, who are Recusants, or who openly or publickly Dissent from the Doctrine, Worship or Discipline of the Church of England by Lawe now Established. Otherwise I should be ready, according to your Lordship's said Order and Injunction, to use my utmost endeavour in Conferring with any such persons, and in using such Arguments and Motives which, by the blessing of God, might be helpfull for the Reducing of them to a right understanding and Perswasion. And I humbly beseech your Lordship to accept of what I have here presented, in Answere to the said Injunction, which your Lordship was pleased to lay upon Your Lordship's most humble and devoted Servant

Henry Gregory[178]

Middleton Stony[179]   July 8, 1682

f.29   MONGEWELL

My Lord,
In obedience to your Lordship's command at your visitation, I have sent this account as to the dissenters from the church, that I have not one in my parish of any sort whatsoever. That all parishes in your Lordship's diocese, and the whole kingdome, may become as free of them, that we may with one mind, and one mouth glorifye God, is the hearty wish and prayer of
My Lord, your most obedient son and servant   N. Davies[180]
Mungell[181]   June 20.   82

f.30a   ROUSHAM

My Lord,
In obedience to your Lordship's late command at Witney in your tryenniall visitation I present you with this followinge account, that we have but one dissenter in our parish, who is a quaker and gardner to my Patron Mr. Dormer.[182] I have frequently had discourse with him aboute his principles,[183] but especially when I first discerned him to be goinge of from our communion, for I thought the sooner the better, and endeavoured accordinge to my ability his conviction, but seeinge all such paines fruitless, I tooke occasion to preach upon some points that he and I cheifly insisted upon, for feare he should leaven any of the rest of my flocke, and sent him in Writinge a briefe account of what I had delivered in publicke

and withall sent him word that if he received noe satisfaction thereby if he would please to send me in Writinge some of his strongest arguments which enduced him to embrace that opinion I should endeavour to answer them, which was accordingly done on both sides, but he remaines still the same, and your Lordship cannot forgett but that you have youselfe had some private discourse with him at Mr. Dormers house, but all proves still ineffectuall, and what further course to take I know not. I question not but your Lordship knowes the obstinacy of that sort of people. I shall give your Lordship noe further trouble at present, but humbly beg your prayers and blessinge for

Your Lordship's most obedient son and humble servant

Richard Dutton[184]

Rowsham[185]   July 15. 1682

He was presented at the last visitation, his name is Robert Dolly

f.30b   SALFORD[186]

Salford   June 07   —82

My Lord,

In the world nothing is more easy then to say our prayers, and to obey our superiours, but yet in the world their is nothing to which we are so unwilling as to prayer, and nothing seems so intolerable as obedience, for I have seen the very baggage of mankind, men that have done things so horrid, worse then which, the sun in all his course never saw, pretending conscience against obedience, expressly against St. Paul's doctrine, teaching to obey for conscience sake. I am sure I am never wise in any thing, but when I obey, for then I have the wisdom of my superiour either for my warrant, or my excuse. My Lord your command is both my warrant and my duty, to give you an account of the state of my litle flock, sheep though they are animalia gregalia, yet they are errabunda exceding subject to stray, if not tended and kept in the better, I have not one that straggles from the fold of our Church, though I have to neer a neighbourhood with them, that endeavour to corrupt their minds from the simplicity that is in Christ, believing our holy Church that she commands artolatry, Christ being no manner of way present in the holy Eucharist, whereas their may be observed four kinds of truths of Christ his presence in the Sacrament, a truth of representation, of revelation, of obsignation, and of exhibition. These are they that have such tender stomacks, that cannot endure milk, but can very well digest iron, consciences so tender that a ceremony is deadly offensive, but rebellion is not. A surplice, like a formidable mormo, frights them from our Church-Communion, but their consciences can suffer them to despise government, to curse all that are not of their opinion, to disturb the peace of kingdomes, and to account schisme the character of saints. My Lord, to the cure of these men, anodynes and softer usages have yet proved ineffective, and unles the lancet be used, we cannot hope to keep our flockes within our inclosures. God in mercy reunite all our divisions, and chang all our mutinous spirites into a sweet Christian temper of gentleness and peace, that with one heart and voice we may serve and praise him in his holy Church: unto this shall tend all the labours, for this shall contend all the prayers of

Your Lordship's most obedient servant   Alexander Charnelhouse.[187]

f.31   SARSDEN

My Lord,
I have a little parish, and I thank God but few dissenters, and that's the true reason of the slowness of my obedience to your Lordship's order, given in your last visitation. We have but two persons that ever frequented conventicles, viz. Susanna the wife of Richard Wansel,[188] and Susanna the wife of William Tidmarsh.[188] There is also another person, Thomas Churchil,[188] who dos very rarely come to Church. And with submission to your Lordship's judgment, I conceive that one line or two from your Lordship's hand to Sir W. Waller[189] for the levying of 12d a Sunday would presently make all these persons perfectly conformable to the Church and its laws, or at least so far as we can judg by their outward Actions.[190]

I am, my Lord, your Lordship's most humble and faithful servant

George Vernon[191]

Sarsden[192]   June 17.   82

f.32   SPELSBURY

My Lord,
In obedience to your Lordship's Command, as well as in Performance of my owne duty, I have discourst 4 Persons (for they are noe more that I can heare of) who are dissenters in the Parish of Spelsbury, two of whom I take to be Anabaptists (or that way inclinable) but the other two I am ignorant under what denomination to place them. Their names are Nicholas Taylor and Alice his wife,[193] Anne Scott widow and William Pufford. They are at present refractory, but I am not out of hopes of reclaiming two of them. I have not one Person in my owne Parish of Heythrop who absents from Church, but cannot yet prevaile (though I was in some hopes at Easter) with William Poltin and his wife to be

participers of the Sacrament of the Lord's Supper.[194] What your Lordship judges requisite to be done further in either Parish, shall be (according to my Power) punctually performed by him who is, my Lord, Your Lordship's most humble and obedient son and servant,

Robert Vicaris[195]

Spelsbury[196]   June the 10th. 1682

f.33   SOUTH WESTON

Weston[197]   June 9th. 1682

May it please your Lordship,

According to your Lordship's command, this is humbly to give your Lordship an account of the seperatists in my Parish, and of my discouse with them. I have one family of Quakers[198] in my Parish, which are all the schismaticks in it. I have discoursed with the master of the family; it would be too tedious and impertinent to give your Lordship a particular relation of such pittifull stuffe, and so I shall onely humbly present to your Lordship the heads thereof. I desired to know of him the cause of his seperation and apostacy. When, after a tedious preamble, he found fault with paedobaptisme, and indeed all baptisme, except his own notionall baptisme with the holy ghost and with fire, railing (after their usuall manner) against baptisme, calling it a cousening or deceiving of children, he spoke a great deale to noe purpose. I told him that he showed himselfe to be a slanderer in calling baptisme a cheate or deceit without any proofe, and that tho paedobaptisme was not expressly commanded in scripture in soe many letters and syllables, yet by undeniable consequence it might be proved out of scripture, which I did indeavour to doe, but without any success as to him. And then in the next place he began to talke against our worship in generall. I desired him to descend to some particulars, but in vaine; here his discourse also was tedious and impertinent, but I observed the thing which troubled him most was the execution of the penall laws. I told him that as master of his family he expected obedience from his wife and children and servants (when he had any) in lawfull things, and so much more ought he to be obedient to the king who is the common father of his people, to which he answered he was obedient; but he did soe mince and limitt his obedience that I could make nothing of it. It was much against his humour that the magistrate should medle with the worship of God. I told him that unless it were soe, I doubt God would be slenderly worshipped, and Atheisme, superstition and profaneness would abound; and here he seemed to agree with me; and I hoped he would not helpe to keepe up the division, but returne into the armes of his mother the church, who would willingly receive him and all her disobedient children; but here he started back quickly, his conscience would not lett him doe that. I told him he must endeavour to gett his conscience rightly informed, and not call interest and faction conscience, but humbly examine himselfe, setting aside all by-respects for his condition seemed to me to be dangerous; for he said if he did conforme, he should sin against his conscience, and I added if he did not returne, he sinned also, in being a schismatic, for schisme is reckoned among the workes of the flesh, which exclude from the kingdome of heaven Gall. 5. to which he had litle to say, but (according to his accustomed manner) left the question in hand, and began to instruct me, for he had a teacher within him (the spirit) which he must follow, and noe other; to which I answered, he ought to examine and try the spirits, and not call his idle fancies motions of the holy spirit; nor his corrupt affections spirituall; for they seemed rather to be carnall, inasmuch as they were swollen with pride, extolling themselves and condemning all others that are not of their perswasion; and God's spirit was a spirit of concord and unity. I desired him also to take heed that he followed not too far that teacher within him; for he that will onely learne of himself (and not have an eare open to the wholesome councell of others, when offered) may have a foole, if not a deceiver to his master. Att last I desired him seriously to consider of it as a weighty business, which concerned the wellfare of his soule; that schisme is a worke of the flesh and excludes from the kingdome of heaven; and that without sin he could not seperate from the church of England, unless he could prove the said church to be idolatrous, or teach any doctrine contrary to the word of God; to which he said nothing to the purpose, but returned againe to his conscience. But I have bin too tedious, for which I beg your Lordship's pardon. To conclude, therefore, your Lordships knows the quakers to be a sort of obstinate and selfe-willed people, but I finde these with whom I have to doe a litle more civill then they have beene formerly. I hope, therefore, your Lordship will pardon this imperfect account which is in all humility presented to your Lordship, knowing that I have to doe with unreasonable men. I heartily wish your Lordship might have received a better account from My Lord, the meanest of your Lordship's curates and servants   Tho. Thomlinson.[199]

f.35 WOODEATON

There is not any recusant or dissenter in the parish of Woodeaton, who does not receive the communion once a year at least, according to the appointment of the church of England.

John Smith,[200] Rector of Woodeaton.[201]

July 29. 1682

f.36 WORTON

Over Worton.²⁰² June 10th, 82.

Right Reverend,

In obedience to your Lordship's command at your last visitation I am to give you an account of the dissenters in my parish of Over Worton which are five woemen in 4 distinct families, persons of inferiour ranke, little sence and I hope noe bad influence, they seeming weary of their ways, and (as many others already) onely ashamed to returne. Two have bin anciently Quakers, a 3d ownes and pleads for that sect, but there is hopes of her returne, a 4th was bred an Independent but these follow noe meetings, and their onely pretext is the vitiousnes of others. The other hath sometimes frequented the Anabaptist meetings, since the late times of Indulgence, their friends haveing bin anciently of that perswasion. Tho' heretofore they baptized a child, according to the custome of our church. And the man begins againe to come to our church-service.

3 of the Quakers children I baptized uppon my first comeing thither, whoe continue of good report in our church. It would bee impertinent to tell your Lordship what ways and meanes I have used to reduce these and withhold others in times of generall toleration. I shall allways labour to strengthen, not weaken the hande of Authority, and desire to live noe longer than I shall conscientiously follow these your Godly admonitions.

There is one more whoe pretends to our communion that hath bin the greatest prejudice and obstruction to mee and my ministery. Hee was accidentally the witnes that appeared against mee in the reference I had heretofore before your Lordship etc. A man that in times of sequestration raised himselfe uppon the plunder of my predecessour, and whoe hath bin a plague to the Neighbour-hood and a scandall and stumbling to the weake. I have often privately admonished, and forgave him my personall wrongs and if I had not timely hindred hee might have forsworne himselfe againe, and came under the hands of publick justice together with all his family, servants etc. within these few weekes. This is the 2d time hee hath layn at my mercy and I have had noe other argument to forgive and spare him but that I might bee assured I could forgive an enemy. I pray God grant your Lordship may never bee soe imposed on againe. But that all your good intentions, and endeavours may meet with answerable effects, to the removeing of whatsoever gives just offence, and to the uniting and healing of this poore distressed church, soe prayeth hee whoe is your Lordship's,

In all duty bounden, Th. Bill.²⁰³

There are noe dissenters belonging to the chappelrie of Netherworton.

II
FELL'S QUERIES AND HIS ARCHDEACON'S REPLIES, 1682

[Fell's queries after his triennial visitation of 1682, addressed to Timothy Halton, Archdeacon of Oxford (MS. Oxf. Dioc. b.68, ff. 9–10).]

(f.9)   In The Deanery of Witney

1. Be pleasd to enquire of Mr. Thackham[204] whither he reside on his cure.
2. To enquire of Mr. Thorp,[205] if Samuel Pack[206] of Burford[207] who is returnd as the Preacher to the dissenters do continue to keep conventicles, that if he does he may be proceeded against according to law. Also to enquire who of those that are returnd, are most fit to be made examples. Whereas James Mady is presented for making a disturbance in the church, be pleasd to learn, if he has made any satisfaction for his fault.
Thomas Minchin[208]
3. To enquire of the names of the three dissenters returnd at Stanlake,[209] who are returnd without any specification.
4. At South Leigh,[210] there is a teacher of a schole said to be an Anabaptist.   q. the name.
5. At Witney nothing presented as amisse; be pleasd to enquire of the state of the town, and to whom the meeting house belongs;[211] as also whither the seats in the church are so altered as to leave a strait passage up to the chancell.

(f.9ᵛ)   Decanatus Woodstock

1. Q. who is the physician lately come to Cuddington,[212] and whither a Papist, as also what schole mistriss.
2. Q. what Papists at North Aston,[213] the return at the last visitation was omnia bene.
3. Q at Charlbury who is the teacher among the dissenters.[214]

Decanatus Chippenorton

1. Q. at Chippennorton, whither the conventicle be still continued: whither the church wardens of the last year have yet receivd the sacrament.[215]

2. To enquire of Mr. Beckingham of Enstone if he can procure the printed paper dissuading officers from presenting dissenters, which was in the hands of Mr. Busby.[216]

3. Q. How the cure is supplied at Hooknorton?[217]

Decanatus Dedington

1. Q. If Bray Doyly[218] continue to keep his conventicle at Adderbury, on Sundaies and Wenesdaies.

2. If Mr. Wheatly[219] keeps his.

3. If young Mr. Wheatly[220] continues to keep his schole.

(f.10)

Q. if there be no dissenters at Swacliffe, Sibford, Epwell[221] and Wiggington,[222] there being none returnd.

Q. at Tew if Mr. Coxon refrains from marrying without license.[223]

[Bicester Deanery]

Q. at Cotesford concerning the glebe and the church which is said to be much embezled.[224]

Q. at Heiford if John Marsh continue his conventicle on Thursdaies.[225]

Q. at Hardwick who is the patron,[226] and whither B. Moore[227] be qualified to hold two livings, and how long the parsonage house has bin left.[228]

Q. at Islip if Jo. Nicols and Eliz. Austin are married.

Q. at Piddington[229] if the parishioners have chose a minister, and if Mr. Ford[230] be the person upon whom they have pitcht. If he be, he is one that I can not approve of, being well enformed of his insufficiency.

Decanatus Henly

At the time of my visitation, time was desired to put in returns, and lately returns are brought without presenting any thing.[231]

(f.10ᵛ)
Q. at Sondcomb of John Big, charged with incontinence with the wife of Francis Tucker

Decanatus Aston

Q. of Will. Turner[232] a teacher at Aston.

Halton's replies to the bishop's queries (MS. Oxf. Dioc. b.68, ff. 11–12)

(f.11)   Decanatus Witney

1. Mr. Thackham lives for the most part in Oxford where he teacheth school.
2. Sam. Pack continues his meetings at Burford. The fittest persons to be prosecuted among the dissenters are Brooks[233] a mercer (who also preaches at Witney) John Greenaway and Richard Haines. James Mady hath made satisfaction for the disturbance in the church.
3. The dissenters at Stanlake whose names were not specified were formerly returned and stand excommunicate.
4. At Southleigh noe teacher of a school is an Anabaptist.
5. Noe information from Witney.

Decanatus Woodstock

1. At Cuddington Mr. Edwards[234] knows of noe physicion; the millers wife teachs school, and is a very good honest woeman.
2. Noe returne from North Aston, neither did the curate[235] appear.
3. At Charlebury, the dissenters are Quakers, and the teacher is usually a woeman, but what her name is they know not.

(f.11ᵛ)   Decanatus Dedington

1. The curate of Adderbury[236] was not at the Visitation.
Noe dissenters at Swacliffe and Wigginton, Sibford or Epwell.
Noe information against Mr. Coxon of Tew for marrying.

Decanatus Bicester

1. At Cotesford the church is much out of repare, the body wherof ought to be repared by Mr. Lort,[237] and the chancell by the minister. Noe bible nor Common Prayer booke, which ought to be provided by Mr. Lort. The glebe said to be imbezled by Mr. Lort.

2. At Heyford John Marsh doth not continue his conventicle.

3. At Hardwick Mr. Farmer of Tesmore[238] is patron, Mr. Moore did not appeare at the visitation. I have ordered him to be cited to produce his qualification to hold 2 livings. 'Tis betwixt 30 and 40 years since the parsonage house was ruined.

4. At Islip the churchwardens know noe such persons as John Nichols and Eliz. Austen.[239] The curate[240] did not appeare.

(f.12)

5. At Piddington the parishioners have chosen Mr. Ford for their minister and some of the parish will shortly wait upon your Lordship about it. I acquainted them that your Lordship would not admitt him.

Decanatus Henly

From Henly neither the rector nor churchwardens did appear.

Sondcomb, Mr. Everett[241] assured me that John Bigg is not charged with incontinence with the wife of Francis Tucker. He did marry the daughter of Francis Tucker and was supposed to have gott her with child before mariage.

Decanatus Aston

William Turner doth not teach at Aston nor any conventicle now kept there.

III

THE ARCHDEACON'S LIST OF DISSENTERS, 1683

[Timothy Halton's list of the numbers of dissenters presented, with a few other matters, by the churchwardens at his visitation, 1683[242] (MS. Oxf. Dioc. b.68, f. 6).]

Henly and Aston Decanati

    Aston Rowant[243]   3 dissenters
    Adwell[244]   2 quakers
    Berrick[245]   1 quaker
    Bixbrand[246]   3 quakers
    Chynnor[247]   1 quaker
    Henly[248]   Eliz. Edwin a bastard child, Joh. Gillingham reputed father
    Lewknor[249]   1 dissenter
    Northstoke   the tower of the church out of repare, the charge great and liberty not able[250]
    Pirton[251]   1 dissenter
    Stokenchurch[252]   3 dissenters
    Sondcomb[253]   3 dissenters
    Southworton[254]   1 quaker
    Watlington[255]   Mary Hakins, John Grendowne a bastard[256] 13 dissenters

Witney Decanatus

    Astall[257]   2 dissenters
    Alvescott[258]   7 dissenters
    Broughton Pogs   1 dissenter
    Bladon[259]   1 dissenter
    Begbrooke[260]   Thomas Mins not paying church rate
    Broadwell[261]   3 dissenters
    Brise Norton[262]   5 dissenters   Bampton[263]   2 papists
    Burford[264]   6 dissenters   Blackborton[265]   4 dissenters

Combe[266]   1 papist   Clanfield[267]   1 quaker
Cassington[268]   6 dissenters
Ducklington[269]   5 dissenters   Hanborough[270]   1 dissenter
Dunstew[271]   2 dissenters   Sir John[272]   not paying 3
                     quarters of masting due to the inhabitants
Kiddington[273]   16 dissenters
Kidlington[274]   1 quaker
Minster Lovel[275]   2 quaker excommunicate
Rowsham[276]   1 dissenter
Stantonharcourt[277] 3 dissenters
Standlake[278]   4 dissenters
Sandford[279]   5 dissenters
Southleigh[280]   Th. Barford not receiving sacrament at
                     Easter
Steple Barton[281]   9 papists   11 dissenters
Stunsfeild[282]   3 dissenters
Taynton[283]   7 quakers
Woodstocke[284]   1 dissenter

Bicester decanatus

Kirkilton[285]   2 dissenters   a midwife unlicensed
Launton[286]   1 dissenter
Frington[287]   3 dissenters   Goddington[288]   8 dissenters
Hamptonpoile[289]   2 dissenters
Heath[290]   9 dissenters
Lillinstonlovell[291] 3 dissenters excommunicate
Mixbury[292]   church not repared
Somerton[293]   all dissenters excommunicate
Stokeline   bells out of order
Solderne[294]   20 dissenters
Bletchington   tower out of repare   Cottesford[295]   1 papist
Steple Aston[296]   church and tower out of repare. That the
                     chappell[297] adjoining to the chancell
                     decay. The want of lords prayer creed and
                     commandments, Kings armes. Keeping
                     bonds and records for parish money in
                     private hands. Noe sanctus bell as
                     formerly. Noe terrier.
Hampton Gay   churchwardens not swore in

(f.6ᵛ)

Hooknorton[298]   The pulpett, seates, pavements and glass

THE ARCHDEACON'S LIST 39

	windows. an order desired to rebuild — 36 Anabaptists
	14 quakers 3 papists A young man teaches children to read
Barton St. Johns	The chancell out of repare
Barton St. Michaels	The chancell out of repare
Bloxham[299]	Henry Coleman[300] keeps a Conventicle. He was forced to leave Glocestershire and is setled here. 17 dissenters
Chadlington[301]	10 dissenters
Charlebury[302]	5 dissenters
Cornewell[303]	Mr. Kerry Rector for not reparing the churchyard wall
Epwell[304]	7 quakers
Kingham[305]	5 dissenters
Milcombe[306]	10 dissenters
Shipton under Wood[307]	6 dissenters and more in 2 hamlets
Salford[308]	Ed. Heron alias Herald late churchwarden for not giving up his accompts.
Swarford[309]	2 quakers
Swacliffe[310]	11 dissenters
Southnewton[311]	13 dissenters
Great Tew[312]	20 dissenters
Wigginton[313]	11 dissenters
Heddington[314]	1 dissenter
Sandford[315]	2 dissenters. Peter Sayer for not paying his part of a tax to the church
Stanton St. Johns	The wall of the churchyard not repared. Noe hearse cloth
Newnham Courtny[316]	The church not repared. 2 dissenters
Holywell[317]	9 dissenters
St. Clements[318]	2 dissenters
St. Michaels[319]	3 dissenters
St. Peters in the East[320]	3 dissenters
St. Ebbs[321]	2 dissenters
St. Thomas[322]	6 dissenters
Magdalen parish[323]	7 dissenters
St. Giles[324]	10 dissenters. Widow Badger not paying tax to repare church.
St. Martins[325]	3 dissenters
Wolvercut[326]	3 dissenters
Waterperie[327]	4 dissenters

APPENDIX

[The return of conventicles in Oxford diocese, 1669 (Lambeth MS. 951/1, ff. 111–13).]

f.111 Oxford Diocesse
Conventicles
1669

f.112 Parishes & Conventicles in them   Sects

County & Diocese of Oxford

        Henley[328]
1   In the house of Wm. Walters[329]   1   Quakers

2   In the house of Wm. Crace a   1   All other sorts of
    London Vintner, once in 3 Weekes   Sectaries, but chiefly
    or oftener sometimes   Presbyterians

        Tame[333]
3   In the houses sometimes of John   1   Presbyterians
    Burton, sometimes of Wm. Atkins   Anabaptists
    etc   etc

This meeting upon the appearing of the Justices is removed into Buckinghamshire

        Watlington[337]
4   In the house of John Oovey[338]   1   Mixt of Presbyterians
    Fellmonger   Anabaptists
                                            etc

5   In the house of Mary East   1   Sabbatarians who observe
    Widow[339] & sometimes of   the Saturday
    Gregory West[340] Weaver

        Lewknor[341]
6   In the houses of Tho. Stevens,[342]   1   Anabaptists
    Wm. North,[343] Christopher
    North,[344] Mr Huish[345] but especially
    at Wormsley house[346]

APPENDIX

Numbers	Quality & Abbettors	Teachers	
40 or 50	The Principall Frequenters and		1
about 300	Promoters of both these Meetings, are such as were Officers and Soldiers in the Parliament Army[330]	Mr Farington[331] Mr Mayo,[332] Mr John Brice NonConformist Ministers	2
about 200		Mr Swinnock[334] Mr Bennet[335] Mr Clarke[336] NonConformist Ministers	3
	The same Oovey is a Notorious Ringleader	And the same is for the most part the Speaker	4
			5
about 30		Mr Collins Teacher	6

APPENDIX

	Parishes & Conventicles in them		Sects
7	Kingston[347] In the houses of Richd. Chitch,[347] John North,[347] & Mrs Mary North	1	Presbyterians Independents Quakers & Sabbatarians mixt.

f.112ᵛ

8	Warborough[349] At the house of Thomas Gilpin[350] an Olivarian Soldier & great Seducer	1	Quakers Every sunday & somtimes on Weeke dayes
9	At the house of Margaret Hinton[351] on Saturdayes	1	Sabbatarians
10	Kept by John Beesly[352] son of the said Margaret Hinton, at her house, monthly	1	Anabaptists
11	Charlbury[356] In the house of Alexander Harris[356] on Sundayes & Frydays most weekes	1	Quakers
12	At Chadlington in the house of Rob. Clement[357] an old Anabaptisticall Soldier	1	Presbyterians Anabaptists etc
13	Chipping Norton[359] In the house of Josiah Disson,[360] on Sundayes	1	Independents

APPENDIX 43

Numbers	Quality & Abbettors	Teachers	
about 30 or 40		Richd. Chitch, John North, Domestique Teachers. Mr Button & one Belcher[348] Forreiners, who under pretence of receiving Rents come thither and teach	7
		The same Gilpin is for the most part Speaker	8
40 or 50		Stamp a Brasier of Abington & others, Teachers	9
about 100	The same Beesly great Abbettor	Wm. Luggrove of Berwick Tabacco Cutter:[353] John Tomkins Bottlemaker,[354] & John Combes Shomaker[355] both of Abington	10
about 30			11
about 30		The same Robert Clement is for the most part Speaker, And sometime one Dunce[358] an Itinerant NonConformist	12
20 or 30		Their Teacher not certaine But often, one Worden[361] formerly a Shomaker	13

APPENDIX

	Parishes & Conventicles in them		Sects
14	Hooke Norton[362] In the house of James Wilmot[363] on Sunday monthly	1	Anabaptists
15	Milton[366] In the house of Robert Seacole[367] at Shipton under Whichwood Monthly	1	Quakers

f.113

16	Adderbury[368] In the houses of Mr Bray Doyley[369] & sometimes of Wm. Gardner,	1	Sometimes Quakers: Sometimes Presbyterians & Anabaptists
17	sometimes of Widdow Swift[370] Weekely		
18	Tadmerton[374] At the house of Wm. Potter[375] every other Fryday	1	Quakers
19	Suadecliffe[378] In the house of Charles Archer[379] at Burdrop	1	Anabaptists
20	In the house of Tho: Gilks[381] at Sibbord Gore	1	Quakers
21	Bloxham[382] In one Ingrams[383] house once a month	1	Anabaptists
22	In the house of George Ason[384]	1	Quakers

APPENDIX

Numbers	Quality & Abbettors	Teachers	
about 60	Leading persons such as were soldiers under Lambert	James Wilmot, Samuel Wilmot,[364] John Lamley,[365] Teachers	14
80 or thereabout			15
sometimes 200		Mr Wells,[371] Mr Whateley,[372] Mr Newell,[373] NonConformist Ministers	16
			17
about 80	Principall Abbettors are the said Wm Potter, John Gun,[376] Benjamin Ward[377] a Quartermaster in Cromwells Army		18
about 50		The same Archer, and one Willmore[380] of Hooke Norton are the Teachers	19
			20
neither in any considerable Number			21
			22

	Parishes & Conventicles in them		Sects
	Burcester[385]		
23	In the house or Barne of Thomas Harris Baker[386]	1	Separatists of all sorts

In this place they have a Pulpit, Seates & Galleries erected; And are sayd by reason of their Impunity to increase[393]

	Dadington[394]		
24	In the houses of Timothy Bicknell,[395] Widdow Wyer,[396] But most frequently in Mr Whateleys[397] Barne at Hampton On Sundayes	1	Presbyterians

f.113ᵛ

	Brise Norton[398]		
25	In the house of Francis Dring,[399] upon Sundayes once a month	1	Quakers
	North-Leigh[400]		
26	At the house of Tho: Taylour[401]	1	Quakers
	Willcot[402]		
27	In the house of Francis Ambrose	1	Anabaptists
	Coggs[403]		
28	In the house of one Mr Blake[404] of the Fine Office, Once & sometimes twice every Lords day	1	Presbyterians & Independents

APPENDIX 47

Numbers	Quality & Abbettors	Teachers	
100 or 200		Mr Bagshaw,[387] Mr Wells,[388] Mr Swinnock,[389] Mr Dod,[390] Mr Troughton[391] & Mr Whateley,[392] NonConformist Ministers	23
about 40		The sayd Mr Whately is for the most part their Teacher	24
about 100	The said Francis Dring is a great Ringleader of that Sect	And is also himselfe a Preacher	25
60 or more			26
Towards 100	The said Ambrose a great Promoter of such Meetings	One Combes, a Miller of Abington, is their Teacher	27
about 200	Edward Wise,[405] Richd Cruchfeild[406] and the Steward of the said Blake, by the said Blakes encouragment are great promoters of this Meetinge in defiance of authority	The Teachers are a Combination of Non-Conformist Ministers viz Dr Langley,[407] Mr Cornish,[408] Mr Dod,[409] Mr Troughton[410] & Mr Connoway[411]	28

NOTES

I

[1] Bray Doyly became lord of the manor of Adderbury West in 1654. His family was wealthy and his support of the Quakers caused considerable embarrassment to his neighbours. Lord Saye and Sele tried to convince him of the error of his ways, but failed signally; see above, p. xxv. Doyly broke the entail on his estates to be able to leave them to his two Quaker nieces. From 1661, he constantly refused to attend church or to pay tithes, and was at intervals fined and arrested. He died in 1696.

[2] In 1669, the Quakers were reported to meet in Doyly's house, see above, p. 44. In 1675, at his own expense and on his land, he had built a plain one-storied meeting house. The building still stands, and was used for worship until the second half of the nineteenth century; see *V.C.H., Oxon.*, IX, 39–40.

[3] A Presbyterian conventicle was reported in 1669, see above, p. 44. Josiah Cox's house in Adderbury and Samuel Cox's in Milton in the parish were licensed as meeting places in 1672 (Lyon Turner, II, 826, 827). A meeting house was made over to the leading Presbyterians in 1708 by Samuel Cox the elder of Milton, on whose land it had been built. It was in use until the 1840s and demolished in the early years of this century. See *V.C.H., Oxon.*, IX, 39 and A. D. Tyssen, 'The Presbyterians of Bloxham and Milton', *Transactions of the Unitarian Historical Society*, II (1920–22), 9–32.

[4] Thomas Whately (1620–99), graduate of New Inn Hall, rector of Sutton under Brailes in Warwickshire from 1649 until his ejection, when he went to live on the property at Hempton, which he had inherited from his grandfather. His father, an eminent Puritan divine, had been vicar of Banbury from 1611 to his death in 1639. In 1669, Whately was teaching at mixed conventicles in Adderbury and Bicester; the Presbyterians met in his barn at Hempton, see above, pp. 45–47. He was licensed as a preacher and his house as a meeting place in 1672 (Lyon Turner, II, 826–27). In 1690, he was reported to be 'somewhat aged and infirme', but still preaching at Milton and Combe (*Freedom after Ejection*, pp. 85–86). He died in 1669 and was buried in Banbury churchyard.

[5] Probably Samuel Statham, ordained 1660, and lecturer at St Giles Cripplegate. In 1672, licensed as a Presbyterian teacher at Loughborough, but imprisoned for nearly three years in Leicester gaol on cancellation of the King's Indulgence. Settled in Banbury, and preached privately, until his death in 1683 (*Calamy Revised*, p. 460).

[6] 1647–1714. For an account of him, see *DNB*. His 'manifold affaires' were by no means all concerned with this parish, where he was curate for the vicar, William Beau, who had become Bishop of Llandaff in 1679. Parsons was also chaplain to Anne, Dowager Countess of Rochester, Canon of Llandaff, and incumbent of two Buckinghamshire parishes — Shabbington and Waddesdon. From May to July 1680, he was in constant attendance on the dissolute John, 2nd Earl of Rochester and was responsible for his deathbed repentance. Other letters from him to Fell, in Nov. 1683 and Nov. 1684 (MS. Oxf. Dioc. c.650, ff.41–42, 45–46) show that he continued to have problems with his parishioners. In 1684, he presented his churchwardens for failure to provide a Bible, Book of Homilies, and communion rail for the church. In 1687, he became rector of Oddington, Gloucs., and was buried there in 1714. The description of him as 'of Adderbury' on the matriculation of his sons at Oxford in 1697, 1698 and 1709, suggests that he continued to reside here.

[7] 2 Papists and 42 nonconformists in Adderbury, Milton and Bodicote in 1676. The difficulty of defining a dissenter is well illustrated in this letter.

[8] The key role of the churchwarden in presenting dissenters and absenters at the visitations of the archdeacon and the bishop, and in procuring their prosecution in the ecclesiastical courts, is apparent in the attempts of the dissenters here to elect one who would be favourable to their cause.

[9] Sir John Clerke, lord of the manor, died in 1682; see above, p. xxxviii.

[10] It was at his house that a conventicle was reported in 1669; see above, p. 42. He was brought before the archdeacon's court in Feb. 1683, and promised to attend church in future (MS. Archd. pprs. Oxon. c.23, f. 65).

[11] Hugh Hunt of Kingston Blount, died in 1694; a farmer of substance, his goods were then valued for probate at £834 0s 8d (MS. Wills Oxon. 34/4/32).

[12] B. A. Pembroke College, Oxford, 1659; vicar of Aston Rowant from 1663 to his death in 1702.

[13] See above, n. 10.

[14] Yeoman, died 1683. When entering the date of his burial, 6 March, in the parish register, the vicar wrote '*prevaricator*' after Turner's name (MS. D.D. Par. Aston Rowant d.3, f. 55). Archdeacon Halton reported in 1683 that Turner was no longer teaching and that the conventicle no longer met, see above, p. 36. It is interesting that the appraisers of Turner's goods for probate included Richard Chitch and Richard Cooper (MS. Wills Oxon. 175/2/5). For other instances of the close co-operation between dissenters in the parish, in acting as witnesses and appraisers for each other, see below, notes 16, 17, 19. Turner's son, another William, was listed by Fell as an 'absenter' in 1685 (MS. Oxf. Dioc. d.708, f. 166).

[15] Christopher Crook and John Chitch the elder were, like Richard Chitch, brought before the archdeacon's court in Feb. 1683, and promised to attend church in future (MS. Archd. pprs. Oxon. c.23, f. 65).

[16] John North senior was reported as teacher of the conventicle in 1669, see above, p. 43. He was buried in April 1683. His will, made in Nov. 1680, was witnessed by, among others, the two Anabaptists, Richard Chitch and Christopher Crook. He left to his widow, Elizabeth, an income of £10 per annum, and the use of the chamber over the buttery in his house. His son, John, was his residuary legatee and executor. His goods were valued for probate at £206 19s 8d (MSS. Wills Oxon. 143/1/9, c.145, f. 10). John North junior died in 1726 and is described in his will as a maltster (MS. Wills Oxon. 143/3/6).

[17] Died 1694. Fell described him as son-in-law to Richard Chitch (MS. Oxf. Dioc. d.708, f. 166). The probate records describe him as 'chirugeon', and in his will (made in 1693, witnessed by Richard Chitch), he left 'all phisicall bookes, instruments, utensils, drugs, compositions and ingredients' to his son, John. On his death, his goods, listed by the Anabaptists John North and Richard Chitch, were valued at £147 4s 6d (MS. Wills Oxon. 8/2/5).

[18] Died 1704 (MS. Wills Oxon. 78/3/58).

[19] Probably the tailor, who died in 1693, when an inventory of his goods, valued at £16 17s 6d, was made by Richard Chitch. In his will, made in 1693 and witnessed by John, Richard and Lucy Chitch, he made Richard Chitch and Thomas Bennett his overseers (MS. Wills Oxon. 121/1/19).

[20] Henry Bertie, brother of the 1st Earl of Abingdon, commander of the company of militia which marched out of Oxford against the Duke of Monmouth in 1685. He joined the Prince of Orange in Nov. 1688.

[21] Giles Gregory of Caversham, J.P., appears to have been active in using the civil power against dissenters (cf. above, p. xxvi). It was he who, in 1676, had his Quaker tenant, Richard Hollyman, evicted from Cuxham Mill (Besse, *Sufferings*, I, 573–74).

[22] 14 nonconformists in 1676; 3 dissenters in Halton's list, 1683, see above, p. 37. The conventicle does not seem to have survived the deaths of John North senior and William Turner, or the activities of the justices. In 1738, the vicar reported 'we have no Dissenters in the parish except two Anabaptists and have no meeting house' (*Secker Visitation*, p. 11).

[23] The only return of 1682 to survive in the form of a presentment, with no explanatory letter to the bishop. It is in the hand of Thomas Snell, vicar of one portion of Bampton from 1677, and of another from 1684. Son of a Devon clergyman; B.A., Exeter College, Oxford, 1666; B.D. from All Souls College, 1676; Canon of Exeter, 1679 and prebendary, 1701. He resigned the vicarage in 1715 and died in 1718.

[24] A large parish, divided into three portions. It contained the six hamlets of Aston, Cote, Lew, Shifford, Chimney and Brighthampton, as well as the town of Bampton. 52 non-conformists in 1676. Dissent had probably been encouraged by the teaching of Samuel Birch, vicar of one portion, until he was ejected in 1662. He continued to rent the vicarage house and preached there until 1664, when he moved to near-by Shilton. He later set up school for the sons of dissenters at Cote manor house (*Calamy Revised*, p. 56). 12 Protestant dissenters listed, c.1663 (MS. Oxf. Dioc. c.430, f. 38). Only 2 papists listed by Halton, 1683, see above, p. 37. House of Hannah Williams of Cote licensed as a meeting place in 1702 (Oldfield, VIII, 803). In 1738, the two vicars reported that the number of Anabaptists remained constant at about 10 or 12 families, and that there were two families of Quakers who attended the meeting at Alvescot (*Secker Visitation*, p. 13).

[25] Edward Bettres of Weald was one of nine Quakers from Bampton who were fined for attending a meeting in John Wheeler's house in Alvescot in Feb. 1675 (Witney Monthly Meeting, Sufferings).

[26] Henry Wheeler had goods worth 17s. distrained in payment of a fine on him, his wife and two daughters for attending the same meeting.

[27] Probably Richard and Elizabeth Window, who were listed as not attending church, c.1663 (MS. Oxf. Dioc. c.430, f. 38). He was excommunicated in 1664 as an absenter and again in 1665 for refusing to have his children baptized (MS. Oxf. Dioc. c.99, ff. 242, 243).

[28] Probably the same Widow Wates who was listed as not attending church, c.1663, and the Ann Watts who, with her daughter Elizabeth, was described as very poor, and had two smoothing irons, one chair and one tin candlestick distrained in payment of the fine for attending the meeting in Alvescot in 1675 (MS. Oxf. Dioc. c.430, f. 38; Witney Monthly Meeting, Sufferings).

[29] Probably Ruth, the wife of John True, who appeared with him before the archdeacon's court in Oct. 1678 as an 'absenter' (MS. Archd. pprs. Oxon. c.22, f. 51). He was listed as not attending church, c.1663 (MS. Oxf. Dioc. c.430, f. 38).

[30] John Hill was listed as not attending church, c.1663, and excommunicated in 1664 (MS. Oxf. Dioc. c.99, f. 242). He was fined 5s. for attending the Alvescot meeting in 1675. When called before the archdeacon's court in 1684, he explained that he was not satisfied in his conscience touching divine service and the sacraments, and was admonished to attend church and receive Holy Communion (MS. Archd. pprs. Oxon. c.23, f. 77). He was indicted at Quarter Sessions in 1687, where he was described as a comb-maker (Oldfield, I, 9).

[31] William Wise appeared before the bishop's court in Nov. 1662 and Mar. 1663. On the former occasion he was admonished to attend his parish church and to receive Holy Communion; on the latter he explained that he was not yet satisfied in some points of conscience and asked for a longer time to consider the matter (MS. Oxf. Dioc. c.4, ff. 45, 90^v). Pewter worth £1 was taken in payment of the fine on him and his three servants who attended the Alvescot meeting in 1675. He also lost three cows which were taken to pay the fines of poorer Quakers, who had no goods which could be distrained. He died in 1687, when he was described as a yeoman of Lew, and his goods valued for probate at £211 19s. His seal had the motto 'That is now revealed which hath been concealed' (MS. Wills Oxon. 73/2/6).

[32] Fell's diocese book supplies his christian name, John, and lists him as a disssenter still in 1685 (MS. Oxf. Dioc. d.708, f. 87^v).

[33] Warwick had goods worth £11 4s. distrained in payment of his own and poorer Quakers'

fines in 1675. He was cited in the archdeacon's court as absent from his parish church in June 1678 (MS. Archd. pprs. Oxon. c.22, f. 16).

[34] Fell lists three Mrs. Bartletts as dissenters — in 1682 Elizabeth at Lew, and in 1685, Dorothy, wife of Edmund, and Mary, wife of John (MS. Oxf. Dioc. d.708, ff. 88, 87^v).

[35] Fell supplies his christian name, John (MS. Oxf. Dioc. d.708, f. 88). He was listed as not attending church, c.1663 and as excommunicated for the same offence in Apr. 1663 (MSS. Oxf. Dioc. c.430, f. 38; c.99, f. 239^v). He appeared before the archdeacon's court in Nov. 1682 (MS. Archd. pprs. Oxon. c.23, f. 34) and before Quarter Sessions in 1687, when he was described as a collar-maker (Oldfield, I, 9).

[36] Probably Catherine, widow of Mark Brickland, gent., of Aston. He died in Apr. 1680, when his goods were valued for probate at £528 3s. (MS. Wills Oxon. 7/2/2). She is not listed among the dissenters in Fell's diocese book.

[37] Both listed in Fell's diocese book in 1682, but only Margaret, wife of William Willicome listed in 1685 (MS. Oxf. Dioc. d.708, ff. 89, 87^v).

[38] Listed by Fell in 1685 as the wife of Robert Oak (MS. Oxf. Dioc. d.708, f. 87^v).

[39] Listed by Fell in 1685 as Robert Evans of Aston (MS. Oxf. Dioc. d.708, f. 87^v).

[40] Fell supplies their christian names, Edward Feild, William Skinner, John Sidwell, and describes the two latter as 'atheists' (MS. Oxf. Dioc. d.708, f. 88).

[41] Listed by Fell in 1682 and 1685 as Robert and Bridget Winterbourne of Weald (MS. Oxf. Dioc. d.708, ff. 88, 87^v). He appeared before the archdeacon's court in June 1678 and before Quarter Sessions in 1687 as an absenter (MS. Archd. pprs. Oxon. c.22, f. 16; Oldfield, I, 9).

[42] The Quakers provided money for the Turner's son, Walter, to be apprenticed to a narrow-weaver of Drayton in 1677 (Witney Monthly Meeting Minute Book). Both John and his wife, Lucy, are listed by Fell (MS. Oxf. Dioc. d.708, f. 90). Both appeared at Quarter Sessions in 1687, charged with not attending their parish church (Oldfield, I, 9). Other shepherds and herdsmen seem to have found it difficult to combine their work with regular attendance at church. William Drinkwater of Gagingwell and Thomas Stranke of Milcombe, when charged in the bishop's court in 1670 as absenters from church, both pleaded their calling as their excuse (MS. Oxf. Dioc. c.11, ff. 9^v, 47).

[43] John Monk recovered from his illness, and in 1683 married Joan Chessus, a Quaker widow of Clanfield (Witney Monthly Meeting Minute Book). Both were charged with being absent from their parish church at Quarter Sessions in 1687 (Oldfield, I, 9). The will of Thomas Monk of Filkins, wheelwright, dated 25 Aug. 1685 'according to the computation of the Church of England' as he put it, was proved in Apr. 1686 (MS. Wills Oxon. 45/3/19).

[44] Jeremiah Bates, B.A., Christ Church, 1668, presented to this living, 1680, resigned it, 1690.

[45] The parish does not seem to have had many dissenters. 2 reported in 1676; 4 in 1683, see above, p. 37. The Quakers attended the meeting at Alvescot (Witney Monthly Meeting Minute Book). In 1738, the vicar reported that there were no Protestant dissenters (*Secker Visitation*, p. 17).

[46] William Beau, Bishop of Llandaff from 1679 and vicar of Adderbury.

[47] Robert Parsons, curate of Adderbury, see above, p. 48 and n. 6.

[48] Matriculated at Corpus Christi College, Oxford, 1650, curate of Bloxham from 1663 to his death in 1696.

[49] Between 1663 and 1665, 23 inhabitants of Bloxham were excommunicated for absenting themselves from church, and two of them for having conventicles meeting in their houses (MS. Oxf. Dioc. c.99, ff. 240^v–43). Two conventicles, one Anabaptist and one Quaker, reported in 1669, see above, p. 44. In 1676, 80 nonconformists in Bloxham and 20 in Milcombe chapelry; 17 dissenters in 1683, see above, p. 39. 10 inhabitants of Bloxham and 6 of Milcombe excommunicated in 1684 as dissenters (MS. Archd. pprs. Oxon. c. 121, f. 28). The house of Thomas Rundle was licensed as a meeting place in 1737 (Oldfield, VIII, 807). In 1738 the incumbent reported 30 Presbyterians, 11 Anabaptists and 8 Quakers in Bloxham, and 5 Quakers, 2 Anabaptists and 1 Presbyterian in Milcombe. There were Baptist meeting

houses in both Bloxham and Milcombe, and a Presbyterian one in Bloxham. The Quakers no longer met in the parish, but travelled to the meeting at Adderbury (*Secker Visitation*, p. 22).

[50] 1 papist and 3 nonconformists in Chalgrove, 8 nonconformists in Berrick Salome in 1676. Halton listed 1 Quaker in 1683, see above, p. 37. Fell listed 2 Quakers in 1685 (MS. Oxf. Dioc. d.708, f. 169). By 1738, only one family of Sabbatarians in the parish (*Secker Visitation*, p. 38).

[51] Fell listed Joseph Wise and his wife as 'Jews' in 1682 (MS. Oxf. Dioc. d.708, f. 168). Their house was licensed as a meeting place in 1700 (Oldfield, VIII, 803). In 1738 the vicar reported that there was one family of Sabbatarians at Berrick, called Wise, at whose house Sabbatarians from the surrounding villages met (*Secker Visitation*, p. 38).

[52] Edward Stennett (d. 1691) moved to Wallingford in about 1658, and occupied rooms in the ruins of the castle. Soon afterwards he was summoned to appear at Newbury assizes, but as a result of numerous accidents, which were seen as the work of divine providence, his prosecutors and their witnesses were prevented from attending, and he was acquitted. He took out a licence for the castle as a Baptist meeting place in 1672. His conventicle, and an off-shoot at Watlington, were still meeting in 1690 (*Baptist Quarterly*, n.s. XIV, 1951–52, 165).

[53] Stephen Coven, ejected from the rectory of Sampford Peverell in Devon, took out a licence to preach in Watlington, as an Independent, in 1672 (*Calamy Revised*, p. 139; Lyon Turner, II, 829). In Sept. 1675 and May 1678, he was presented by the churchwardens of Dorchester for not coming to church and for keeping a conventicle 'contrary to the laws of this land' (*Oxon. Peculiars*, pp. 127, 128).

[54] Fell listed a John Benham or Binham in 1682 and 1685 (MS. Oxf. Dioc. d.708, ff. 168, 169).

[55] B.A., Magdalen Hall, Oxford, 1658; vicar from 1668 to his death in 1701; from 1676 also rector of Little Shelford, Cambs.

[56] This letter provides the most detailed list which has survived among the answers to Fell's instructions at his visitation, see above, p. xxxi. Most of the people listed here do not occur elsewhere as dissenters; those who do are noted below.

[57] The Blounts of Mapledurham, a staunchly Catholic family, had suffered much for their loyalty to the King during the civil war (*Catholic Missions*, pp. 319–21). Elizabeth was the wife of William Blount of Mapledurham and Kidmore End, who died in 1676. They were both, with their nephew Walter (the head of the family) and his wife, among those presented for not attending church, c.1663 (MS. Oxf. Dioc. c.430, f. 42). Walter, on his death in 1671, left the Mapledurham estate to Elizabeth and William's son, Lyster. Elizabeth was listed by Fell as a Papist in 1685 (MS. Oxf. Dioc. d.708, f. 154).

[58] Charles, younger son of Elizabeth and William, died in 1691.

[59] Probably a relative of Elizabeth Blount, who was daughter of Sir Ralph Delaval of Seaton Delaval, Northumberland. A Robert Delaval was listed by Fell as a Papist in 1685 (MS. Oxf. Dioc. d.708, f. 154).

[60] For another example of a parish constable who was not a conforming member of the established church, see above, p. 4.

[61] Both listed by Fell as Quakers, with their wives, in 1685 (MS. Oxf. Dioc. d.708, f. 154).

[62] John Fitzgerald, 18th Earl of Kildare (1661–1707), bought Caversham House from the Earl of Craven. His successor sold it to Earl Cadogan in 1718.

[63] The underlining perhaps means that he attended conventicles.

[64] See above, p. 49 and n. 21.

[65] In 1738, the minister pointed out that many of the houses in the parish were 'a great distance from the church' (*Secker Visitation*, p. 34).

[66] B.A., Christ Church, 1672; probably left Caversham in 1684, when he became rector of Finedon, Northants. and of Woodford, Essex.

⁶⁷ i.e., Caversham. 2 Papists and 2 nonconformists in 1676. In 1738, no Papists or Quakers, 2 Presbyterians and 1 Anabaptist (*Secker Visitation*, p. 35).

⁶⁸ i.e., Leafield, in the parish of Shipton under Wychwood, where a Quaker conventicle was reported in 1669, see above, p. 44. Both Leafield and Milton under Wychwood were centres of Quaker activity. Milton was one of the four preparative meetings of the Witney monthly meeting in the 1670s, and a separate preparative meeting was established at Leafield in 1678 (Witney Monthly Meeting Minute Book). 42 nonconformists in Shipton parish in 1676. Seven of the Quakers were excommunicated in 1684 (MS. Archd. pprs. Oxon. c.121, f. 28). The Quaker meeting house in Milton was still active in 1738 (*Secker Visitation*, p. 134).

⁶⁹ See below, p. 62, n. 215.

⁷⁰ Son of Edward Coles, a farmer in Bletchingdon; B.A., Pembroke College, Cambridge, 1673; ordained at Ely, 1675; at his institution to the vicarage of Charlbury in 1681, described as 'late of the cathedral church of Ely'; resigned the living in 1690.

⁷¹ The town had a long history of Quaker dissent, starting with the conversion of Anne Downer, the daughter of a former vicar of Charlbury (*V.C.H., Oxon.*, x, 153). In 1663 and 1664, 22 inhabitants were excommunicated for not attending church (MS. Oxf. Dioc. c.99, ff. 237–44). A mixed conventicle reported in 1669, see above, p. 42. 2 Papists and 48 nonconformists in Charlbury and 15 nonconformists in Chadlington in 1676. During the 1670s the Quakers attended Milton under Wychwood meeting. Their own meeting house was built in 1681, and by 1689 had a burial ground (*V.C.H., Oxon*, x, 153). Fell copied the minister's return of 25 dissenters into his diocese book, and in 1685 listed 26 dissenters, 11 of them different names from the 1682 return (MS. Oxf. Dioc. d.708, ff. 118, 117ᵛ). In 1738 the curate reported 22 Quakers and 1 family of Presbyterians (*Secker Visitation*, p. 37).

⁷² Harris was the leader of the Quakers in the parish. It was at his house that the conventicle met in 1669, see above, p. 42, and he was the chief promoter of the building of the meeting house in 1680 (Witney Monthly Meeting Minute Book). He had been imprisoned in 1657 for 3½ years for refusing to pay tithes (Besse, *Sufferings*, I, 564). He and his wife, Mary, were excommunicated in 1663 (MS. Archd. pprs. Oxon. c.121, f. 80). In 1684, goods of his worth £8 were distrained by the constables of Charlbury to pay a fine on Milton meeting house, of which he was a trustee — a position he gave up in 1689, to make way for a younger man (Witney Monthly Meeting Minute Book).

⁷³ Grace, wife of Thomas Busby, was buried 22 Feb. 1698. The vicar annotated the entry in the parish register 'Quaker' (MS. D.D. Par. Charlbury c.1, f. 85ᵛ).

⁷⁴ Henry Shod and his wife, Elizabeth, were excommunicated in 1663 (MS. Oxf. Dioc. c.6, f. 33) and in 1667 (MS. Archd. pprs. Oxon. c.121, f. 80). When summoned to the archdeacon's court he refused to take off his hat, and, when ordered not to continue teaching school, replied that he would not observe that command (*V.C.H., Oxon.*, II, 49). Henry was buried 5 May and Elizabeth 26 Nov. 1684 (MS. D.D. Par. Charlbury c.1, f. 85ᵛ).

⁷⁵ Possibly Francis Strange who, with his wife, was excommunicated in 1663 (MS. Oxf. Dioc. c.99, f. 240) and was listed by Fell in 1685 as Francis Strank (MS. Oxf. Dioc. d.708, f. 117ᵛ).

⁷⁶ Listed by Fell in 1685 as Richard (MS. Oxf. Dioc. d.708, f. 117ᵛ).

⁷⁷ Excommunicated in 1684 and listed by Fell in 1685 (MSS. Archd. pprs. Oxon. c.121, f. 28; Oxf. Dioc. d.708, f.117ᵛ).

⁷⁸ With Clare and Carpenter presented to the archdeacon's court in Feb. 1684, but not excommunicated (MS. Archd. pprs. Oxon. c.23, f. 66).

⁷⁹ Possibly Elizabeth, wife of John Miles, yeoman, who died in 1687 (MS. Wills Oxon. 141/2/19).

⁸⁰ Possibly Anne White who was excommunicated in 1670 (MS. Archd. pprs. Oxon. c.121, f. 76).

⁸¹ Mary Harris and Thomas Grant were excommunicated in 1667; both the Harris's and Richard Brooks appeared before the archdeacon's court in 1668, admitted not receiving

Holy Communion at Easter, but promised to receive it at Whitsun (MSS. Archd. pprs. Oxon. c.121, f. 76; c.17, ff. 143, 143^v). Harris, Grant and Brooks were summoned to the bishop's court in 1675 (MS. Oxf. Dioc. c.13, ff. 18, 19).

[82] Richard Harris, farmer, was brought before the bishop's court in Oct. 1668 and excommunicated; in 1671, he asked for the excommunication to be lifted and for time to attend his parish church (MSS. Archd. pprs. Oxon. c.17, f. 196^v; Oxf. Dioc. c.11, f. 167^v). He may be the Richard Harris who died in 1703 and whose goods were valued for probate at £430 9s 4d (MS. Wills Oxon. 167/4/5).

[83] Thomas Packford was licensed as a Baptist teacher and Thomas Crasse's house as a Baptist meeting place in 1672 (Lyon Turner, II, 830).

[84] B.A., University College, Oxford, 1654; rector from 1657 to his death in 1683.

[85] No Papists or nonconformists in 1676. In 1738, the rector thought the good order and uniformity of the parish in great measure due to the care and good example of the two principal families of Greenwood and Jones (*Secker Visitation*, p. 40).

[86] Mary Gom was excommunicated in 1662 (MS. Oxf. Dioc. c.99, f. 238^v). The churchwardens' accounts note the payment of 1s. 'for a distresse to distreigne' Richard Gomme in 1683 (MS. D.D. Par. Chinnor d.1, f. 57).

[87] William Paul, Bishop of Oxford from 1662 to 1665, and rector of Chinnor, where he died in 1665.

[88] Rector from 1669 to 1691, when he was succeeded by his son, Charles. He published *Daniel in the Den* (London, 1682), a discourse on Hebrews, XI. v. 33, dedicated to the Earl of Shaftesbury on his deliverance from the machinations of the papists, who would have made him out a traitor.

[89] 2 nonconformists in 1676; 1 Quaker in 1683, see above, p. 00. The house of Richard King was licensed as a meeting place for Baptists in 1732 (Oldfield, VIII, 806); yet the rector reported that there were no dissenters in 1738 (*Secker Visitation*, p. 44).

[90] The top right hand corner of the letter is missing.

[91] Vicar from 1671 to his death in 1731. In 1674 he subscribed as a schoolmaster (MS. Oxf. Dioc. e.22, p. 20).

[92] 3 nonconformists in 1676; 1 Quaker in 1683, see above, p. 38; no dissenters in 1738 (*Secker Visitation*, p. 46).

[93] An Oxfordshire man, his father was of Witney; B.A., Corpus Christi College, Oxford, 1637; rector of Stonesfield from 1662 to his death in 1705; curate of Combe from 1663.

[94] 1 Papist in Combe and 1 Papist and 6 nonconformists in Stonesfield in 1676; no dissenters in 1738 (*Secker Visitation*, p. 153).

[95] George and Robert Weston were excommunicated in 1663 (MS. Archd. pprs. Oxon. c.121, f. 363). George was committed to Oxford gaol on a writ *de excommunicato capiendo* and kept there for 8 years (Besse, *Sufferings*, I, 570).

[96] All the Quakers, except Elizabeth Weston and Alice Laughton were listed by Fell in 1685 (MS. Oxf. Dioc. d.708, f. 113^v).

[97] Alice Hurst appears to be a convert to Catholicism, unlike most of her faith who, when brought before the ecclesiastical courts, usually pleaded as their excuse that they had been brought up in the Catholic faith.

[98] The Rector of Cornwell, in replying to the Bishop's request for information about dissenters, did not confine himself to the problem of dissent. As a result, his letter is to be found in MS. Oxf. Dioc. c.650, among the general correspondence of the Bishops of Oxford relating to parish affairs. It provides an extreme example of poor relations between the incumbent and the principal landowner of a parish. Sir Fairmedow Penyston (1656–1705) succeeded his brother in the baronetcy in 1679. His father, Sir Thomas, 2nd Bart., as deputy lieutenant of Oxfordshire was considered a 'bitter persecutor of Dissenters', see above p. 25.

[99] Matriculated, Christ Church, 1656; rector from 1672 until he resigned the living in 1689.

[100] No dissenters in 1676, or, despite the rector's forebodings, in 1738 (*Secker Visitation*, p. 47).
[101] For Whately, see above, p. 48 and n. 4.
[102] The house of Philip Ordoway was licensed as a meeting place in 1707 (Oldfield, VIII, 804).
[103] John and Timothy Bignell and John Appletree, when brought before the archdeacon's court in Dec. 1684, refused to answer the presentment, 'it being too general' (MS. Archd. pprs. Oxon. c.23, f. 85ᵛ). For Timothy, see below p. 72 and n. 395.
[104] Probably John Rowse, baker, who died in 1686 (MS. Wills Oxon. 172/5/18).
[105] Probably William Rowse, yeoman, brother of John, who died in 1685, and left three tenements with lands in Deddington (MS. Wills Oxon. 56/5/15).
[106] William Rowse (see above, n. 105), in his will, left £5 to Mary Makepeace whom he described as 'the child who is with me'.
[107] Thomas Owen of Hempton died in 1706, his widow in 1718 (MSS. Wills Oxon. 171/2/6 and 143/5/9).
[108] Anthony Prentice, yeoman of Clifton, who died in 1684. His will, made in 1681, was witnessed by William and Elizabeth Rowse (MS. Wills Oxon. 52/3/30). The death of his wife Anne in 1678 is recorded in the Quaker register (O.R.O., BMM III/5).
[109] Fell noted in his diocese book that Mr. Whately was an unlicensed teacher (MS. Oxf. Dioc. d.708, f. 129). Probably as a result of this letter, Samuel Whately was brought before the archdeacon's court in Nov. 1682, charged with teaching school 'without licence lawfully obtained from his Bishop'. He did not obey the order to stop teaching, and was before the archdeacon again in June 1684 (MS. Archd. pprs. Oxon. c.23, ff. 32, 78).
[110] B.A., Sidney College, Cambridge, 1672; vicar from 1673 to his death in 1697. In 1678 he also served as curate of Barford St. Michael, and from 1682, he taught boys in Deddington (perhaps an attempt to counteract the influence of the nonconformist school). Between 1689 and 1697, he made numerous efforts, through the ecclesiastical courts, to force his reluctant parishioners to pay him tithes and Easter offerings.
[111] The presence of two nonconforming ministers (Thomas Whately at Hempton, and, from 1665 to 1672, Samuel Wells, the ejected vicar of Banbury) encouraged the growth of a Presbyterian congregation in the parish. About 40 people attended it in 1669, see above, p. 46. In 1672, three houses (of Philip Appletree, Timothy Bignell and Thomas Whately) were licensed as Presbyterian meeting places (Lyon Turner, II, 826–27). 35 nonconformists in 1676. After the Toleration Act, no fewer than five houses in the parish were licensed as meeting places — those of Francis Clanfield, carpenter in Clifton in 1706, Philip Ordoway in 1707, Richard Maynard in Clifton in 1722, Thomas and John Fardon for the Quakers in 1731, and Anthony Harris in 1737 (Oldfield, VIII, 804, 806, 807; MS. Oxf. Dioc. c.644, item 1). The number of dissenters remained more or less constant. In 1738, there were 28 Presbyterians, 2 Anabaptists, 7 Quakers and 2 families of Papists (*Secker Visitation*, p. 53).
[112] For George Ashwell, rector of Hanwell, see below, p. 57, n. 136.
[113] Fell supplies their christian names, William and Elizabeth (MS. Oxf. Dioc. d.708, f. 130).
[114] For the problem of labelling those who attend both parish church and conventicles, see above, p. xix. The Presbyterian conventicle flourished in Banbury from 1672, when three houses were licensed as meeting places and two men, Samuel Wells and James Sutton, as preachers (Lyon Turner, II, 826; see above, p. xxi). After the death of Wells in 1678, the conventicle continued to attract people from all over the Banbury area. In 1718, a newly-built meeting house in the Horse Fair was licensed (Oldfield, VIII, 804). In 1738, 50 Presbyterian families (*Secker Visitation*, p. 14). The Quaker conventicle also flourished (see above, p. xxiv).
[115] He was probably too ill to travel to Oxford to see the bishop himself. He died in June 1683, having been rector here since 1679. In his will, he left 20s. to the poor of Drayton, two theological works and a bible to his nephew, and the residue of his estate to his sister. His goods were valued for probate at £99 10s, including £26 for his books (MS. Wills Oxon. 45/3/12).

[116] Despite the proximity of Banbury, the rectors of Drayton do not appear to have been troubled with many dissenters. None in 1676; in 1738 'but one Presbyterian' (*Secker Visitation*, p. 54).

[117] Between 1662 and 1665 six parishioners of Duns Tew were excommunicated for being absent from church (MS. Oxf. Dioc. c.99, ff. 238^v–243^v). In 1676, 9 nonconformists. In 1702, the house of James Castle was licensed as a dissenting meeting place (Oldfield, VIII, 803). No dissenters of any kind in 1738 (*Secker Visitation*, p. 56).

[118] Abraham Dawes and Jonas and Sarah Smalbone had been excommunicate since the early 1660s (MS. Oxf. Dioc. c.99, ff. 238^v, 242^v). Dawes was buried in the parish churchyard, 29 Sept. 1682 (MS. D.D. Par. Duns Tew c.1, f. 12). The Smalbones were still listed by Fell as dissenters in 1685 (MS. Oxf. Dioc. d.708, f. 109).

[119] B.A., Wadham College, Oxford, 1669; vicar from 1676 to 1690, when he became rector of Jevington, Sussex. In 1684, he was licensed to teach boys in Duns Tew.

[120] Annotation in Fell's hand.

[121] The influence of William Burnet, ejected from the vicarage here in 1662, perhaps encouraged dissent. 10 nonconformists in 1676; but none in 1738 (*Secker Visitation*, p. 59).

[122] Possibly the Quaker Mary Ryton, who was fined £5 in 1662 for attending a meeting (Besse, *Sufferings*, I, 568). Her influence on her daughters, Mary and Elizabeth, may well have been underestimated. They both married dissenters — John and Timothy Bignell of Deddington — and were left £100 each in their father's will (MS. Wills Oxon. 57/1/12).

[123] Plot gives an account of these waterworks in his *Natural History of Oxfordshire* (Oxford, 1705), pp. 241–44.

[124] Before the archdeacon's court in July 1671, Edward Busby admitted not attending church as often as he should, because of the distance of his house from the parish church. His reason for not receiving Communion at Easter was also the common one of being in London on business (MS. Archd. pprs. Oxon. c.19, f. 150).

[125] See above, p. xxxix.

[126] Probably son of William Beckingham of Charlbury, who graduated from Magdalen College, Oxford, in 1639. Presented to the living in 1645, sequestered in 1654, and restored in 1660; died here in 1682.

[127] Admitted to the living in 1648. In 1649, with Samuel Wells, he presented to Fairfax a petition of ministers around Banbury deprecating proceedings against the King. Probably sequestered during the civil war, but restored about 1660 (*Walker Revised*, p. 30). He was still rector of Fringford at his death in 1697.

[128] Fringford had a small number of dissenters, both Protestant and Catholic throughout the second half of the seventeenth century. Two of its inhabitants were excommunicated in 1663 for not coming to church, and 1 in 1664 (MS. Oxf. Dioc. c.99, ff. 240^v, 241^v). 3 Papists and 2 nonconformists in 1676. Only one Catholic and no other dissenters in 1738 (*Secker Visitation*, p. 65).

[129] Excommunicated in 1680 (MS. Archd. pprs. Oxon. c.121, f. 121). Listed by Fell as a dissenter in 1685 (MS. Oxf. Dioc. d.708, f. 140). Buried in the parish churchyard, 16 Jan. 1694 (parish register).

[130] Excommunicated as a 'reputed Anabaptist' in 1664 (MS. Oxf. Dioc. c.99, f. 241^v). Still listed by Fell as a dissenter in 1685 (MS. Oxf. Dioc. d.708, f. 140). Perhaps the John Payne, 'a poor man', buried in the parish churchyard, 19 Feb. 1706 (parish register).

[131] With his wife, Anne, excommunicated in 1680 (MS. Archd. pprs. Oxon. c.121, f. 121). Both still listed by Fell in 1685 (MS. Oxf. Dioc. d.708, f. 140).

[132] Manuscript torn.

[133] For Fell's use of St Cyprian's discourse, see above, p. xxxi

[134] Calthorpe House was the meeting place of the Presbyterian conventicle in Banbury; see above, n. 114 and *V.C.H., Oxon.*, x, 112.

[135] Abiezer Coppe (1619–72), a notorious fanatic, in turn Presbyterian, Anabaptist and

Ranter, preached in Warwickshire and the surrounding area, including Hook Norton and Burford, in the 1640s. For an account of him, see *DNB*.

[136] 1612–94. For an account of him, see *DNB*. He had been an undergraduate, fellow and sub-warden of Wadham College, Oxford, until expelled from the university in 1648. Rector of Hanwell from 1658 to his death. His *Fides Apostolica*, published in 1653, was a defence of the Apostles' Creed. His *Gesta Eucharisticus*, published in 1663 and dedicated to his patron, Sir Anthony Cope, was a defence of the ceremonies of the Anglican church, which emphasized his view that there could be no unity in the church without uniformity of ritual. His will contains a lengthy preamble thanking God for making him not only a member, but also 'a Steward of some part of this his family in the Church of England, which I have always esteemed, as It stands now by Law established, to be not only an Orthodox and Regular Church in Its own constitution, but withall the best and purest part of the Catholick that I know; as being the most conformable to the Rule of holy Scripture; as also to the Doctrine and practice both, of the primitive Church in Its first and purest Ages, whether wee respect the publick worship, or Its own Government and Discipline. Christian, is my Name; and Catholick, my Surname. By which Titles I profess an utter Detestation, both of all Heresies which have corrupted the faith; and of all Schismes, which have confounded the Peace of the Christian Church; yet withall bearing an unfeined pity towards the persons of the seduced, and praying for their Conversion'. He made elaborate arrangements for his books to be listed, for copies of the catalogue to be circulated in and around Oxford, and for the books to be sold 'according to such prices as they would yeeld in the shops, or not much short of them' (MS. Wills Oxon. 2/2/29).

[137] There is little evidence of dissent in Hanwell. This was probably in large measure due to the combined efforts of Sir Anthony Cope, the lord of the manor, and of Ashwell, who, as well as being devoted to the Anglican faith, was (as this letter suggests) a conscientious parish priest. 2 parishioners were excommunicated for not attending church in 1664 (MS. Oxf. Dioc. c.99, f. 242). 1 nonconformist in 1676. 1 Anabaptist in 1738 (*Secker Visitation*, p. 71).

[138] Fell lists Richard Haiward and his wife as absenters (MS. Oxf. Dioc. d.708, f. 155^v).

[139] B.A., Lincoln College, Oxford, 1632; B.D., 1642; expelled by the Parliamentary Visitors in 1648. This experience may explain his harsh attitude to the nonconformists. Rector of Harpsden (and of Whitwell, Derbs.) from 1662 to his death in 1687.

[140] 2 parishioners, Edward Bush and John Round, excommunicated in 1663 for not attending church (MS. Oxf. Dioc. c.99, f. 239^v). 3 nonconformists in 1676. 3 families of Presbyterians in 1738, including that of the lord of the manor (*Secker Visitation*, pp. 73–74).

[141] The Fermor family of Tusmore was staunchly Catholic. They owned large estates in the north-east of Oxfordshire, especially in Somerton, Godington, Hardwick and Tusmore. They favoured Catholic tenants and servants, and the chapel at Tusmore served as a place of worship for the surrounding area (*Secker Visitation*, p. 135). In 1682 Richard Fermor was head of the family. He died in London in 1684, but his body was brought back to be buried among his ancestors in Somerton parish church (*Catholic Missions*, pp. 66–79).

[142] Fell's diocese book supplies the wife's name, Ann (MS. Oxf. Dioc. d.708, f. 144^v). She was still listed as a reputed Papist in 1706 (Hassall, p. 78).

[143] Fell supplies the wife's name, Margaret (MS. Oxf. Dioc. d.708, f. 144^v). Both were excommunicated in 1680 (MS. Archd. pprs. Oxon. c.121, f. 144). Their daughter, Elizabeth, administrator of her father's goods in 1696 (MS. Wills Oxon. 166/3/14), married Henry Bennett, a carpenter, and, with him, was listed as a Papist in 1706 (Hassall, p. 78).

[144] Margaret Newton was excommunicated in 1680 (MSS. Oxf. Dioc. d.708, f. 144^v; Archd. pprs. Oxon. c.121, f. 144).

[145] Listed as a Popish recusant, *c*.1663 (MS. Oxf. Dioc. c.430, f. 40).

[146] Excommunicated in August 1680 (MS. Archd. pprs. Oxon. c.121, f. 144).

[147] Fell listed 16 'absenters from sacraments' in the parish (MS. Oxf. Dioc. d.708, f. 144^v).

[148] For other examples of incumbents who advocated the enforcement of the penal laws against dissenters, see above, p. xxxvii.

[149] Hugh Boham of Harpsden also advocated prayer and fasting, see above, p. 20, as did Fell in his sermon to the House of Lords on 22 Dec. 1680, a day of 'solemn humiliation'.

[150] Probably the Richard Evans who was B.A. from Magdalen College, Oxford in 1641. Rector from 1662 to his death in 1699. His goods were valued for probate at £219 6s 9d, which included £3 for a 'study of bookes' (MS. Wills Oxon. 79/2/38).

[151] The parish, encouraged by the Fermor family, had a long tradition of Catholicism. 3 were reported, c.1663 (MS. Oxf. Dioc. c.430, f. 40), 10 in 1676, 5 in 1706 and 5, with 5 children in 1738 (Hassall, p. 78; *Secker Visitation*, p. 77).

[152] This letter provides an extreme example of the problem of passive neglect of church atttendance, as distinct from active dissent and attendance at conventicles. Much of the cause seems to lie in the very poor relations between the incumbent and his parishioners, but it is interesting that some gave the Popish tendencies of the Anglican church as the reason for their absence from its services.

[153] Sir Henry Allnut was, from 1650, owner of the Ibstone House estate (*V.C.H., Bucks.*, III, 63). His attitude to his family's and his neighbours' neglect of worship is in interesting contrast to his prosecution of the Quakers and Sabbatarians in Lewknor, see above, p. 26. For other examples of the influence of local landowners on religious practice in their parishes, see above, pp. xxv, xxviii.

[154] Fell supplies the name of the papist — Catherine Atkins — and of the Sabbatarians — Thomas and Hannah Cook (MS. Oxf. Dioc. d.708, f. 172).

[155] Bishop of Oxford from 1665 to 1671.

[156] For the use to which Fell hoped this tract would be put, see above, p. xxxi.

[157] Disputes concerning non-payment of tithes, or the method of payment (whether in kind or in money) were normally settled in the ecclesiastical courts. Only disputes over the ownership of tithes would have been a matter for the common law courts. The usual problems of collecting tithes from parishioners reluctant to pay them, may have been exacerbated for Richard Parr by the geographical position of his parish, detached from the rest of the diocese, and surrounded by parishes in the jurisdiction of the bishop of Lincoln. (I am grateful to Dr D. M. Barratt for elucidation of the problems of tithes in this letter.)

[158] Possibly sainfoin, which from the 1660s had been introduced into England as a good fodder-grass to cultivate on poorer soils.

[159] The different customs about where payment was to be made, when animals were not pastured for the whole year in the same parish, were a source of infinite disputes.

[160] The white tithe was payment in money instead of milk.

[161] The commutation of payment in kind into a money payment per acre of land, regardless of the use to which the land was put, was a normal arrangement in many parishes. Here, the parishioner appears to have fixed his own sum at too low a rate.

[162] B.A., Brasenose College, Oxford, 1660. Rector of Ibstone from 1665 to his death in 1708. Peter Shelley of Caversham was similarly disliked by his parishioners for his excessive zeal in carrying out Fell's instructions, see above, pp. 9–10.

[163] There is not much evidence of active dissent in the parish. 2 Papists and 4 nonconformists in 1676; no dissenter of any sort in 1738 (*Secker Visitation*, p. 85).

[164] Only occasional inhabitants of Islip were dissenters in the period. John Hawkes was excommunicated in 1664 for not attending church, and Mary Bolt in 1665 as a papist (MSS. Archd. pprs. Oxon. c.121, f. 223; Oxf. Dioc. c.99, f. 243^v). 1 Papist in 1676 and 3 in 1706 (Hassall, p. 78); no dissenters of any sort in 1738 (*Secker Visitation*, p. 87).

[165] B.A., Corpus Christi College, Oxford, 1669; ordained deacon, 1673; B.D., 1682; rector of Hampton Poyle from 1683 to his death in 1693.

[166] Only one inhabitant of Kencot appears in the records as an active dissenter — Thomas Monk, who was excommunicated in 1663 for 'willfully absenting himself from church' (MS.

Oxf. Dioc. c.99, f. 240ᵛ). This is probably the wheelwright who was a Quaker in Filkins in 1682, see above, p. 51 and n. 43.

[167] One of the more unusual reasons given for not attending church; for another see above, p. 12. In 1738, the curate of Hethe thought that 'poorness of dress and laziness' were the main reasons why some parishioners never came to church (*Secker Visitation*, p. 77).

[168] B.A., Balliol College, Oxford, 1666; rector from 1666 to his death in 1702.

[169] An Anabaptist conventicle met here in 1669, see above, p. 40. Thereafter the number of dissenters declined. 8 nonconformists in 1676, 1 in 1683, none in 1738 (see above, p. 37; *Secker Visitation*, p. 97).

[170] For the variation in the enforcement of the penal laws, see above, p. xxv.

[171] See above, p. 58, n. 153.

[172] See above, p. 49, n. 21.

[173] The Anabaptist conventicle met in their house in 1669, see above, p. 40. They appeared before the bishop's court in 1666 and were admonished to attend their parish church (MS. Oxf. Dioc. c.9, f. 42ᵛ). In the archdeacon's court, in Feb. 1684, they admitted being Anabaptists, and promised to attend church in future (MS. Archd. pprs. Oxon. c.23, f. 65).

[174] This hope was not fulfilled. William North was still at Moor Court, Lewknor, when he died in 1693. He left his son 12d, and the bulk of his lands and money to his wife, to go, after her death, to their grandson. His goods were valued for probate at £620 14s. (MSS. Wills Oxon. 143/1/22; c.145, f. 58).

[175] Compare the comments of the rector of Ibstone on the problem of neglecters, p. 22.

[176] For the importance of the role of the churchwarden in the presentation of dissenters, see above, pp. xxxviii–xxxix.

[177] B.A., All Souls College, Oxford, 1661; vicar from 1666 to his death in 1715. In his will, made in 1711, he directed that all his 'sermon notes, manuscripts, letters, papers and writings whatsoever' be burned at his death (MS. Wills Oxon. 116/3/41).

[178] An Oxfordshire man, matriculated at Christ Church in 1644, expelled by the Parliamentary Visitors in 1648, returned to proceed B.A. in 1650, and M.A. in 1653. Rector from 1662 to his death in 1689. The lengthy preamble to his reply to the bishop gives a clear account of Fell's instructions, see above, p. xxxi.

[179] James Farren was ejected from the rectory in 1662, but does not seem to have left any parishioners who shared his dislike of the re-established church. No dissenters were reported in 1676 or in 1738.

[180] Nehemiah Davies graduated from Jesus College, Oxford, in 1667. Rector from 1671 to 1684, when he moved to Compton, Berks.

[181] There is no evidence of the small parish of Mongewell being affected by dissent in this period, except for one Papist in 1676.

[182] Robert Dormer, who bought the manor of Rousham and built the house there. He died in 1689.

[183] Robert Dolly is an interesting example of an individual dissenter who resisted all attempts to convince him of the error of his ways, despite his apparent isolation in the parish. He died in 1715 (MS. Wills Oxon. 125/1/5). The burial, in the Quaker burial ground at Adderbury, of Isabell Baritt, maidservant to Mr Dormer, was recorded in 1678 (O.R.O., BMM III/5).

[184] Matriculated at Balliol College, Oxford, 1652; presented by Robert Dormer to the rectory in 1658; on his death in 1690, he was succeeded by his son, Ellis.

[185] Rousham never seems to have had more than one or two nonconformists in the period. Fell listed Dolly's wife with him as a dissenter (MS. Oxf. Dioc. d.708, f. 111ᵛ). In 1738, one old woman, a Quaker, was the only dissenter (*Secker Visitation*, p. 128).

[186] Despite its proximity to Chipping Norton and the conventicles there, Salford does not appear to have been troubled with dissenters in this period.

[187] B.A., Pembroke College, Oxford, 1650; rector from 1660 to his death in 1710. During the 1690s, he was in dispute with his churchwarden, John Kite, over numerous matters,

including Kite's non-attendance at church, and responsibility for repairs to the parsonage house (MSS. Oxf. Dioc. c.92, ff. 1, 13; c.50, f. 40).

[188] None of the three appears in other records as a dissenter. The conventicles at Chipping Norton and Chadlington may have tempted them away from their parish church.

[189] Sir William Walter and his wife were recorded by the Quakers as having beaten and abused Ellis Hookes, because he would not take off his hat to them (Besse, *Sufferings*, I, 564).

[190] For other incumbents who shared this view, see above, p. xxxvii.

[191] 1637–1720. For an account of him, see *DNB*. In his *Ataxiae Ostaculum* (London, 1677) he attacked the dissenters' plea of conscience as a reason for their schism, and strongly supported the use of the civil power to enforce conformity, see above, p. xxxix. Rector from 1663 to his death in 1720; also rector of Bourton on the Water, Gloucs., and of St John and St Michael in Gloucester.

[192] There is no further evidence of dissent in the parish in this period.

[193] Excommunicated in 1663 for refusing to have his children baptised (MS. Oxf. Dioc. c.99, f. 240).

[194] The only example in these letters of people who attended church, but had scruples about taking Holy Communion. A husbandman of Dunthrop in Heythrop, William Poltin was buried 19 Oct. 1689. His goods were valued for probate at £310 18s 10d (MS. Wills Oxon. 144/4/38).

[195] B.A., St Alban's Hall, Oxford, 1662; rector of Heythrop from 1675 to his death in 1704. The incumbent of Spelsbury had been deprived of the living. Vicaris probably took care of the parish until the new rector was appointed in May 1683. In 1690 and 1691 Vicaris was at odds with his churchwarden, John Cox, whom he presented for various offences, including absence from church services and failure to produce accounts at the end of his term of office. Cox in turn presented the rector, for, among other things, residing outside the parish (at Chipping Norton), and for keeping the parish register there (MS. Oxf. Dioc. c.93, ff. 260, 262). In 1738 the rector reported that he lived at Chipping Norton 'as all my predecessors have done' (*Secker Visitation*, p. 82).

[196] There is no other evidence of dissent at Heythrop in this period. 2 nonconformists in Spelsbury in 1676.

[197] South Weston, in Aston deanery. Only two families of Quakers appear in the parish in this period, see below, n. 198. No dissenters in 1738 (*Secker Visitation*, p. 140).

[198] Presumably Richard and Elizabeth Hollyman, who were, with Alice Green, presented by the churchwardens for not attending church, in July 1679 and again in Sept. 1681 (MS. Oxf. Dioc. b.68, ff. 1, 2). Fell listed the Hollymans' son and daughter with these three as Quakers in 1682 (MS. Oxf. Dioc. d.708, f. 177). In 1685 Fell only listed Alice Green; probably by then the Hollyman family had moved to Adwell mill (*V.C.H., Oxon.*, VIII, 15; cf. below. p. 64, n. 244).

[199] This is the longest account given in these letters of a discussion between an Anglican clergyman and a dissenter. It illustrates well the lack of common ground between the disputants. Thomlinson was curate of Forest Hill in 1670 and rector of South Weston from 1672 to his death in 1689. Probably B.A., Queen's College, Oxford, 1658.

[200] B.A., Balliol College, Oxford, 1660; fellow of Magdalen College; D.D., 1681; rector of Woodeaton from 1680 to his death in 1690. His will (proved in the Chancellor's court, Hyp. B. 33) refers to his 'chamber at Oxford', where he probably spent much of his time. He asked his executors to burn all his sermon notes and 'all other writings whatever under my own hand' within a month of his death.

[201] There is no evidence of dissent in the parish during this period.

[202] Over Worton had been a centre of dissent in the 1670s. The house of John Higgins was licensed as a meeting place in 1672 (Lyon Turner, II, 828). 10 dissenters in 1676. As this letter suggests, by 1682 their numbers were dwindling. No Protestant dissenters in 1738 (*Secker Visitation*, p. 179).

II

²⁰³ B.A., Wadham College, Oxford, 1657; rector of Over Worton from 1664 to his death in 1683. An indication of the conformist principles of the parishioners is given in the presentment of their rector in 1667, for administering the sacrament without wearing a surplice (MS. Top. Oxon. c.56, f. 82).

²⁰⁴ Thomas Thackham, vicar of Broadwell and rector of Nuffield, from 1668 to his death in 1690.

²⁰⁵ John Thorp, vicar of Burford from 1669 to his death in 1701.

²⁰⁶ Samuel Pack was brought before the archdeacon's court in Nov. 1682 and excommunicated in Dec. (MSS. Archd. pprs. Oxon. c.23, f.34; c.121, f. 54).

²⁰⁷ There were both Presbyterians and Quakers in Burford. A Quaker meeting in the town was broken up and 7 men arrested in 1662 (Besse, *Sufferings*, I, 569). 11 people were excommunicated in 1663, 3 in 1664, and 3 in 1665 for not attending their parish church (MS. Oxf. Dioc. c.99, ff. 239ᵛ–42ᵛ). Abraham Drye, ejected rector of Great Rissington, Gloucs., was preaching in Burford, Brize Norton and the surrounding area in the 1660s (*Calamy Revised*, p. 171). 21 nonconformists in 1676. Fell listed 25 in 1682 and 8 in 1685 (MS. Oxf. Dioc. d.708, ff. 93, 92ᵛ). Halton noted 6 in 1683, see above, p. 37. In 1695 the house of Samuel Wheeler was licensed as a Quaker meeting place, and in 1710 that of Joseph Robbins (sect unspecified) (Oldfield, VIII, 802, 804). The present Quaker meeting house was opened in 1708 or 1709. In 1738, the vicar reported 13 Presbyterians, Independents and Anabaptists, who met in the same meeting house, and 12 Quakers (*Secker Visitation*, p. 32).

²⁰⁸ In the MS. Minchin's name is written in the margin. He was a mercer in Burford, the leading Quaker in the town, who suffered much for his dissent. He was brought before the bishop's court in May 1663 to explain why he did not attend his parish church. He answered 'he doth not allowe of those prayers and soe doth not beleive the same to be a true church' and added 'scandalous speeches' against the vicar. He was excommunicated in October (MSS. Oxf. Dioc. c.6, f. 10ᵛ; Archd. pprs. Oxon. c.121, f. 52). He was sent to Oxford gaol in March 1664, on a writ *de excommunicato capiendo*, and kept there until the King's pardon released him in 1672. His goods were distrained in 1675, in payment of a fine for attending the Alvescot meeting; in 1683, probably as a result of these inquiries, he was imprisoned, as an excommunicate, and kept in gaol for almost 3 years (Witney Monthly Meeting, Sufferings). The Witney Monthly Meeting minute book records, in Nov. 1688, that he bought the ground for Witney meeting house, and provided more than £83 towards the cost of the building. In 1689 he gave up his position as trustee of the meeting house to a younger man.

²⁰⁹ It does not appear that Fell got the information he required (cf. above, p. xxxix and MS. Oxf. Dioc. d.708, f. 100). 6 inhabitants of Standlake were excommunicated in 1662 and 1665 (MS. Oxf. Dioc. c.99, ff. 238ᵛ, 243ᵛ). 5 nonconformists in 1676; 4 noted by Halton in 1683, see above, p. 38. In 1738, 4 Anabaptist families attended the meeting at Cote (*Secker Visitation*, p. 143).

²¹⁰ Fell noted in his diocese book, 2 Quakers, William and Catherine Shepherd, and 2 Anabaptists, William Anker and Thomas Barfoot (MS. Oxf. Dioc. d.708, f. 102ᵛ).

²¹¹ Dissent had probably been encouraged by the teaching of William Gilbert, who was ejected from a lectureship in the town in 1662, but who stayed in the area, and was licensed as a Presbyterian preacher in Stanton Harcourt in 1672. Francis Hubbard, ejected from the vicarage of Winterborne Monkton, Wilts. was in 1672 licensed as a Presbyterian preacher here. His house and that of Charles Wing were licensed as meeting places (Lyon Turner, II, 827). The Anabaptists also had a licensed teacher, John Carpenter, and a meeting house, Widow Colier's, in 1672 (Lyon Turner, II, 830). Witney was the centre of Quaker activity in the west of the county. 15 nonconformists in 1676. So there were grounds for Fell's suspicion of the return that all was well. Dissent continued to flourish. The Quaker meeting house was

completed in 1688. The house of Mr Samuel Mather was licensed as a meeting place in 1703 (Oldfield, VIII, 803). In 1738, 40 families of Presbyterians, Independents and Anabaptists met at the Presbyterian meeting house, and there were 30 families of Quakers (*Secker Visitation*, p. 174).

[212] Encouraged by the Browne family, Catholicism flourished in Kiddington (*Catholic Missions*, p. 123). 9 Papists in 1676. 14 'dissenters' listed by Fell in 1682 (MS. Oxf. Dioc. d.708, f. 107^v), and 16 in 1683, see above, p. 38. 13 Papists plus 20 children in 1706 (Hassall, p. 80), 63, including children in 1738 (*Secker Visitation*, p. 88).

[213] The presence of two strongly Catholic families in the parish, the Annes and the Brookes, ensured the survival of Catholicism into the 18th century (*Catholic Missions*, p. 51). 14 Papists in 1676; 16 in 1706 (Hassall, p. 80); one family in 1738 (*Secker Visitation*, p. 108).

[214] See above, p. 10, for the incumbent's return of dissenters in 1682.

[215] The complaint of the vicar of Charlbury, that dissent in Chipping Norton had a bad influence on his parishioners, probably prompted this inquiry. The vicar of Chipping Norton, Stephen Ford, had been ejected for nonconformity. He continued to live and preach in the town, until, according to Calamy, his life was threatened and he fled to London. His influence, and the fact that the living was vacant from 1663 to 1683, no doubt encouraged the growth of dissent (see above, p. xxviii). An Independent conventicle met in the house of Josiah Diston in 1669, see above, p. 42. The same house was licensed as a meeting house in 1672 (Lyon Turner, II, 828). An indication of the number of the dissenters is given in their application, which was refused, to use the Town Hall as a meeting place. 77 nonconformists in 1676. The Presbyterians had a resident minister in 1690 (*Freedom after Ejection*, p. 85). They took out licences for meeting places for the house of John Thorley in 1722 and the chapel 'lately erected in New Street' in 1736 (Oldfield, VIII, 806, 807). A group of Quakers developed in the town, after a visit by Mary Clark in about 1656. Chief among the Quakers was Giles Tidmarsh, who was excommunicated in 1661, and imprisoned in Oxford gaol until 1672 (MS. Oxf. Dioc. c.99, f. 238; Besse, *Sufferings*, I, 573). The house of Giles Tidmarsh [junior] was licensed as a meeting place in 1703 (Oldfield, VIII, 803).

[216] See above, p. 16.

[217] Fell's desire to discover which of his clergy was responsible for the care of souls in Hook Norton was no doubt a result of concern at the number of dissenters in the parish. 16 people were excommunicated in 1665 (MS. Oxf. Dioc. c.99, ff. 243^v–44). An Anabaptist conventicle met in the town in 1669, see above, p. 44. 90 nonconformists were reported in 1676. Fell listed 41 dissenters (MS. Oxf. Dioc. d.708, f. 121), and Halton noted 36 Anabaptists, 18 Quakers and 3 Catholics in 1683, see above, pp. 38–39. 2 people from the parish had been excommunicated in 1679 and 1 in 1680 (MS. Archd. pprs. Oxon. c.121, ff. 205, 203). Probably as a result of Fell's inquiries, 28 of the dissenters were excommunicated in 1684 (MS. Archd. pprs. Oxon. c.121, f. 28^v). Although Archdeacon Halton did not reply to this particular query, other letters to Fell show that he took appropriate action. Edward Jennings, who had been curate of Hook Norton since 1670 and also curate of Great Rollright, was suspended (MS. Oxf. Dioc. c.650, ff. 31, 48). He was replaced, in April 1683, by Cope Doyley, who had been ordained by Fell in Dec. 1682. Dissent continued to flourish. Houses in the town were licensed as meeting places in 1700 and 1716. In 1719, having disposed of the old meeting house and erected another on part of Mr. William Harwood's estate, the Baptists applied for another licence (Oldfield, VIII, 803, 804). In 1738, there were 18 families of Anabaptists and 14 of Quakers; both sects had meeting houses (*Secker Visitation*, pp. 83–84).

[218] See above, p. 48 and n. 1.

[219] See above, p. 48 and n. 4.

[220] See above, p. 55 and n. 109.

[221] Fell had good reason to be suspicious of a return that gave no dissenters in the parish of Swalcliffe, which included the villages of Epwell, Sibford Gower, Sibford Ferris and Shutford. Conventicles of Anabaptists and Quakers had been reported in 1669, see above,

p. 44. 15 nonconformists in 1676. The women's monthly meeting of the Banbury area Quakers met in Shutford and Sibford and nine other places in the region in rotation from 1677 (O.R.O., BMM I/14). Fell noted in his diocese book that the Quakers met at Sibford Gower every Friday and Sunday, and the Anabaptists every other Sunday (MS. Oxf. Dioc. d.708, ff. 133, 132ᵛ). Halton noted 11 dissenters in Swalcliffe and 7 Quakers in Epwell in 1683, see above, p. 39. In 1684, 5 dissenters of Epwell were excommunicated (MS. Archd. pprs. Oxon. c.121, f. 28). The house of Thomas Nichols in Shutford was licensed as a meeting place in 1705 (Oldfield, VIII, 803). By 1738, the Anabaptists numbered only 2 and had ceased to meet in the parish; there were 28 families of Quakers with meeting houses in both Sibford Gower and Shutford (*Secker Visitation*, p. 155).

²²² Fell noted in his diocese book 'no particular person returned and the paper not subscribed'. Later he added the names of three dissenters there — George Westbury, Thomas Giles and Alice Clifton (MS. Oxf. Dioc. d.708, ff. 133, 134). These three, with John Sturch and Elizabeth Nibb, were excommunicated in 1684 (MS. Archd. Pprs. Oxon. c.121, f. 28ᵛ).

²²³ A memorandum of Jan. 1681 notes that Henry Coxon, curate of Great Tew and vicar of Sandford St Martin, was 'in contumacy for not appearing at the consistory court of the Lord Bishop . . . to answer to certain articles etc. for clandestine marriages in the church of Great Tew' (MS. Oxf. Dioc. b.68, f. 3).

²²⁴ Fell's concern about the preservation of the glebe was reflected in his instructions to the clergy, at his next triennial visitation in 1685, about the making and preserving of glebe terriers (MS. Top. Oxon. c.161, f. 3).

²²⁵ In Feb. 1678, at the Quarterly Meeting of Friends in Oxford, it was decided that a meeting should be held once a fortnight at Lower Heyford (*V.C.H., Oxon.*, VI, 194). Fell listed 16 Quakers in his diocese book and noted that John Marsh kept the meeting on Thursdays in his barn, that he and his wife Deborah had not been legally married and refused to have their son baptised (MS. Oxf. Dioc. d.708, f. 144). Marsh, with Richard Day of Lower Heyford, was excommunicated in 1680 (MS. Archd. pprs. Oxon. c.121, f. 190). It is not clear why the conventicle ceased to meet, but there is no doubt that Quakers continued to live in the parish, though their numbers decreased. Rebecca, daughter of John and Deborah Marsh, described as 'of Lower Heyford', was buried in the Quaker burial ground in Adderbury in 1695, as was John Marsh in 1731 (O.R.O., BMM III/5). By 1738 there was only one Quaker (*Secker Visitation*, p. 80).

²²⁶ Hardwick had a long tradition of Catholicism, encouraged by the Fermor family who were lords of the manor and patrons of the living (*V.C.H., Oxon.*, VI, 169, 173; see above, p. 57, n. 141).

²²⁷ Brian Moore, rector of Hardwick, died 1700.

²²⁸ In 1665, the rector was living in a house with two hearths, but by 1679 the rectory was described as ruinous (*V.C.H., Oxon.*, VI, 169).

²²⁹ Following a dispute between the vicar of Ambrosden and the villagers of Piddington (a chapelry in Ambrosden parish) in the 15th century, the consistory court had decreed that the parishioners of Piddington could elect their own minister (*V.C.H., Oxon.*, V, 256).

²³⁰ John Ford appeared before the bishop's court, charged with preaching at Piddington on 15, 22 and 29 Oct. 1682, though unlicensed, and with disturbing the minister appointed to serve the cure on one of these Sundays. He was forbidden to preach there or in any other parish in the diocese until he had obtained a licence from the bishop (MSS. Oxf. Dioc. c.91, f. 206; Archd. pprs. Oxon. c.23, f. 31).

²³¹ Fell had reason to be suspicious of a return that all was well in Henley. In 1669 there were conventicles of both Quakers and Presbyterian, see above, p. 40. In 1672, the house of William Cornish was licensed as a Presbyterian meeting place. The Congregationalists applied for, but were refused, a licence to use the Town Hall; instead the houses of Thomas Cole and John Tyler, and the barn of Alexander Burnard were licensed as meeting places and Thomas Cole (ejected rector of Ewelme and teacher of a nonconformist school at

Nettlebed) was licensed as a teacher (Lyon Turner, II, 828, 829–30). 76 nonconformists in 1676. Probably as a result of Fell's inquiries, proceedings were taken against 11 of the dissenters, who were excommunicated in 1683 (MS. Archd. pprs. Oxon. c.121, f. 162). Dissent continued to flourish. Mr. Jeremy Froyser had a large congregation in 1690, who paid him £40 *per annum* (*Freedom after Ejection*, p. 85). The house of John Cutler was licensed as a meeting place in 1693 (Oldfield, VII, 802). In 1738 the rector reported that about one third of the parish attended the Presbyterian meeting house; there were about 10 families of Quakers who also had their own meeting house (*Secker Visitation*, p. 78).

[232] Sometime before 3 July 1682 Turner had promised the vicar that he would attend the parish church. He died in March 1683. (See above, p. 49 and n. 14).

[233] Swift action was taken against Joshua Brooks, who was excommunicated on 11 Dec. 1682 (MS. Archd. pprs. Oxon. c.121, f. 48).

[234] Jonathan Edwards, rector of Kiddington, 1666–87.

[235] John Hough (1651–1743) was vicar of North Aston from 1678 to 1687. He was fellow of Magdalen College at this time and must have provided a curate to serve the cure.

[236] Robert Parsons, see above, p. 48 and n. 6.

[237] Laurence Lord leased the manor from Eton College, from 1676 to his death in 1708 (*V.C.H., Oxon*, VI, 106).

[238] Richard Fermor, see above, p. 57 and n. 141.

[239] In his diocese book Fell noted these two as 'clancularly married' in the parish of Lillingstone Lovell (MS. Oxf. Dioc. d.708, f. 146).

[240] Edward Penny, see above, p. 58 and n. 165.

[241] Samuel Everard, rector of Swyncombe from 1666 to his death in 1688.

III

[242] For Timothy Halton, see above, p. xxxiv. This list, which survives among the diocesan papers, was probably Halton's report to Fell of such matters as had been presented as amiss in the parishes he had visited at his Michaelmas visitation in 1683. The list is not dated, but can, on internal evidence, be assigned to late in 1683. Edward Herrell, who was presented at Salford for not providing a statement of his accounts as churchwarden, had been churchwarden in 1681 and 1682 (see below, n. 308). The bastard child of John Grendown, presented at Watlington, was baptised in May 1683 (see below, n. 256). The churchwardens of Steeple Aston appeared before the archdeacon's court in Feb. 1684, to explain the state of their church (see below, n. 297).

[243] See above, pp. 2–5.

[244] In his diocese book in 1685, Fell noted that Richard Hollyman and his family were Quakers in the parish (MS. Oxf. Dioc. d.708, f. 167). He was a miller and had been evicted from Cuxham mill in 1676 (see above, p. 60 and n. 198; *V.C.H., Oxon.*, VIII, 15).

[245] See above, p. 7.

[246] The churchwardens had presented 5 people in July 1679 and in Sept. 1681 for being absent from church or for not receiving communion (MS. Oxf. Dioc. b.68, ff. 1, 2). Fell noted two families of Quakers in 1685 (MS Oxf. Dioc. d.708, f. 154).

[247] See above, p. 11.

[248] Cf. above, p. 63, n. 231.

[249] Cf. above, pp. 25–26.

[250] In July 1679 the churchwardens presented their belfry as out of repair, and in Sept. 1681 their tower 'which we have begun building but are not able to go forward with it without the help of the rest of the parish (MS. Oxf. Dioc. b.68, ff. 1, 2).

[251] 3 nonconformists and 10 Papists in 1676. In 1682 Fell noted in his diocese book that all was well; in 1685 there was one papist and two 'fanatics', William and Christian Gregory (MS. Oxf. Dioc. d. 708, ff. 174, 173^v). The Gregorys were excommunicated in 1663 for refusing to

go to church (MS. Oxf. Dioc. c.99, ff. 239, 241). The house of Sarah Lewinton was licensed as a meeting place in 1719 (Oldfield, VIII, 805).

[252] 12 nonconformists in 1676. Fell listed 3 Quakers and 1 Anabaptist (MS. Oxf. Dioc. d.708, f. 174). The latter, Richard Smith, had been excommunicated in 1662 for refusing to go to church (MS. Oxf. Dioc. c.99, f. 238v). In May 1667 he came before the bishop's court, having suffered the penalty of the law for almost three years since the writ *de excommunicato capiendo* went out against him, said he was sensible of his error, and promised not to attend conventicles and to have his four children baptised (MS. Oxf. Dioc. c.9, f. 159).

[253] The churchwardens presented 4 Papists in 1679 (MS. Oxf. Dioc. b.68, f. 1). The influence of the Fettiplace family encouraged the survival of Catholicism (*V.C.H., Oxon.*, II, 43). 6 Papists in 1706 (Hassall, p. 81); one in 1738 (*Secker Visitation*, p. 157).

[254] i.e., South Weston. See above, p. 60 and n. 197.

[255] Several large groups of dissenters in the parish had come to the notice of the ecclesiastical authorities since 1660. 10 were excommunicated in Jan. and Feb. 1663 for refusing to attend their parish church, 12 in Dec. 1663, and 7 in Feb. and March 1664 (MS. Oxf. Dioc. c.99, ff. 239–41v). 20 were cited in the archdeacon's court in 1668 (MS. Archd. pprs. Oxon. c.17, ff. 95–96). In 1669 there were two conventicles, one Sabbatarian, the other Presbyterian and Independent, see above, p. 40. In 1670 John Richardson was charged in the archdeacon's court with keeping unlawful conventicles in his house. He denied having such meetings 'in these twelve months', and promised to have no more (MS. Archd. pprs. Oxon. c.18, f. 137). In 1672 Steven Coven (see above, p. 52, n. 53) was licensed to teach to a Congregational conventicle in Thomas Ovey's house, and John Harper's house was licensed as a Presbyterian meeting place (Lyon Turner, II, 828, 829). 47 nonconformists in 1676. 13 dissenters listed by Fell in 1685 (MS. Oxf. Dioc. d.708, f. 176v). The decline in numbers continued. In 1738 the vicar reported 'very few Protestant Dissenters' whose number he considered 'dwindled by disregard', though Anabaptists from the surrounding villages still met in the house of Nathaniel Nash, tanner (*Secker Visitation*, p. 163).

[256] A very rubbed entry in the parish register records the baptism on 29 May 1683 of John 'the reputed son of John Grendown' (MS. D.D. Par. Watlington b.2, f. 15v).

[257] Fell listed 5 papists and 7 Anabaptists in 1682, 1 Papist and 1 Anabaptist in 1685 (MS. Oxf. Dioc. d.708, ff. 86, 85v).

[258] 11 nonconformists in 1676. Fell listed 6 Anabaptists in 1682 (MS. Oxf. Dioc. d.708, f. 86v). In 1678 the Quakers decided to establish a regular meeting at Alvescot. Meetings had already taken place in the parish. In 1675, 29 Quakers from Alvescot, Bampton, Witney, Burford and Milton under Wychwood were fined for attending a meeting here (Witney Monthly Meeting, minute book and sufferings). The meeting house was still active in 1738, though only one of the congregation lived in Alvescot (*Secker Visitation*, p. 7).

[259] Fell noted that there were 2 dissenters, Thomas and Elizabeth Slater, in 1682, and queried whether Mistress Slater was a schoolmistress (MS. Oxf. Dioc. d.708, f. 106v).

[260] There is no evidence of dissent in the parish in this period.

[261] 4 Papists and 4 nonconformists in 1676. 7 dissenters in 1682 and 3 Quakers in 1685, listed by Fell (MS. Oxf. Dioc. d.708, ff. 91, 90v). 4 Papists in 1706 (Hassall, p. 80).

[262] A Quaker conventicle met here in 1669, see above, p. 46. 7 nonconformists and 4 Papists in 1676. Fell noted Francis Dring, Quaker, and Joshua Harris, Anabaptist in 1682 and 1685 (MS. Oxf. Dioc. d.708, ff. 98, 99). In 1738, 2 Presbyterian families, with no meeting house, no Quakers (*Secker Visitation*, p. 27).

[263] Cf. above, p. 5.

[264] See above, p. 61, n. 207.

[265] Cf. above, pp. 5–6.

[266] Cf. above, pp. 12–13.

[267] Cf. above, pp. 11–12.

[268] 4 Papists in 1676. The Reynolds family was persistently Catholic. Christopher Reynolds came before the archdeacon's court in 1671 and 1681; both times he admitted that he had

been brought up as a Catholic and was allowed time 'better to inform himself' (MSS. Archd. pprs. Oxon. c.19, ff. 153^v, 185^v; c.23, f. 9). Fell listed him and two other Papists in 1682 and 1685 (MS. Oxf. Dioc. d.708, ff. 107, 106^v). In 1682 he also listed three Anabaptists, two of whom were excommunicate. Edmund and Ann Reynolds were listed as Papist in 1706 (Hassall, p. 80). There were 'three or four' Papists in 1738 (*Secker Visitation*, p. 34).

[269] 1 Papist and 3 nonconformists in 1676. 3 Quaker women appeared before the archdeacon's court in 1678 (MS. Archd. pprs. Oxon. c.22, f. 51). These three, with two others, were listed by Fell, who also noted the presence of one Papist in the parish (MS. Oxf. Dioc. d.708, ff. 95^v, 96). Two reputed Papists in 1706 (Hassall, p. 80). By 1738, only two Anabaptists (*Secker Visitation*, p. 55).

[270] Robert Rogers had been ejected from the rectory in 1662 and had moved away from the area (*Calamy Revised*, p. 415). A small number of dissenters throughout the period. 1 Papist and 1 nonconformist in 1676. Fell listed 1 Papist and 1 Anabaptist (MS. Oxf. Dioc. d.708, ff. 109^v, 110). 4 Papists in 1706 (Hassall, p. 80). 'Very few' dissenters in 1738 (*Secker Visitation*, p. 70).

[271] Cf. above, p. 15

[272] Blank in the MS.

[273] Cf. above, p. 62, n. 212.

[274] There is evidence of a small but persistent number of Quakers in the parish. John Sims was excommunicated in 1662 (MS. Oxf. Dioc. c.99, f. 238). 3 listed by Fell (MS. Oxf. Dioc. d.708, ff. 110^v, 111).

[275] Two Anabaptists, William Thomas and Roger Williams, were excommunicated in 1663 (MS. Oxf. Dioc. c.99, f. 239). 16 parishioners were presented as absent from church in 1668 (MS. Archd. pprs. Oxon. c.17, ff. 94, 94^v). William Thomas and Roger Williams, with other members of the Thomas family, were listed by Fell in 1685 (MS. Oxf. Dioc. d.708, f. 97^v).

[276] Cf. above, pp. 27–28.

[277] Sir Philip Harcourt (M.P., died 1688) had Presbyterian ministers as his chaplains — notably Henry Cornish in the 1660s and 1670s (see above, p. xvi); but he does not appear to have encouraged the growth of dissent in the parish. In 1672 Cornish and William Gilbert were licensed as Presbyterian teachers (Lyon Turner, II, 827). 5 nonconformists in 1676; 4 listed by Fell (MS. Oxf. Dioc. d.708, ff. 116, 117).

[278] Cf. above, p. 61, n. 209.

[279] 4 inhabitants of the parish excommunicated in 1663, one as a Quaker (MS. Oxf. Dioc. c.99, f. 240). 13 Papists and 6 nonconformists in 1676. Fell noted only 1 dissenter in 1685 (MS. Oxf. Dioc. d.708, f. 113^v). 1 reputed Papist in 1706 (Hassall, p. 81). 1 Presbyterian and 1 Papist in 1738 (*Secker Visitation*, p. 129).

[280] Cf. above, p. 61 and n. 210. It was Thomas Barfoot who applied, in 1697, for the house of Ann Bullock to be registered as a meeting place (Oldfield, VIII, 802).

[281] The parish had persistent groups of Quakers and Papists in the period. 9 Papists, 5 of them in the household of Edward Sheldon, *c.*1663 (MS. Oxf. Dioc. c.430, f. 38). Fell listed 10 in 1682, 4 in the household of Ralph Sheldon (MS. Oxf. Dioc. d.708, f. 106). 9 reputed Papists in 1706 (Hassall, p. 81); none in 1738, probably because the Sheldon family, though still lords of the manor of Suswell's Barton, had moved into Warwickshire (*Secker Visitation*, p. 149). Fell listed 11 Quakers in 1682, 7 of them of the Fletcher family, 2 of whom had been excommunicated in 1663 (MSS. Oxf. Dioc. d.708, f. 106; c.99, f. 240).

[282] Cf. above, pp. 12–13.

[283] There is evidence of a small group of Quakers in the period. 6 were excommunicated in 1663 for not coming to church, and 1 for not paying a church rate (MS. Oxf. Dioc. c.99, f. 240^v). Three of the same were listed, with three more, by Fell in 1682 and 1685 (MS. Oxf. Dioc. d.708, ff. 102, 103). 6 nonconformists in 1676.

[284] Two houses were licensed as Presbyterian meeting places in 1672 (Lyon Turner, II, 828). 1 Papist and 1 nonconformist in 1676. Fell did not list any dissenters in his diocese book (MS. Oxf. Dioc. d.708, f. 115^v). In 1738, the vicar of Bladon considered that 'there were

NOTES TO THE ARCHDEACON'S LIST

formerly in Woodstock a pretty many Presbyterians and Independents; but they have been decreasing of late years, as in most other places' (*Secker Visitation*, p. 18).

[285] i.e., Kirtlington. 1 Papist and 4 nonconformists in 1676. Fell listed 3 dissenters in 1685 (MS. Oxf. Dioc. d.708, f. 145^v).

[286] 2 inhabitants of Launton excommunicated in 1664 (MS. Oxf. Dioc. c.99, f. 241^v). 1 Papist in 1676; 1 noted by Fell in 1682 (MS. Oxf. Dioc. d.708, f. 146^v).

[287] i.e., Fringford, see above, pp. 17–18.

[288] These dissenters were probably Papists, of whom 4 were excommunicated in 1663 (MS. Oxf. Dioc. c.99, f. 240). 15 Papists in 1676; 12 listed by Fell in 1682 (MS. Oxf. Dioc. d.708, f. 141); 14 in 1706 (Hassall, p. 78). The increase in the number of Catholics, no doubt the result of the Fermor family being lords of the manor, alarmed the vicar in 1738 (*Secker Visitation*, p. 68).

[289] 1 nonconformist in 1676; 2 listed by Fell in 1682 (MS. Oxf. Dioc. d.708, f. 141^v).

[290] See above, pp. 21–22.

[291] 4 nonconformists in 1676. Fell listed 1 Quaker and 5 'absenters' in 1682 (MS. Oxf. Dioc. d.708, f. 146).

[292] Mixbury church suffered severe storm damage in 1662, and at some time in the 17th century was extensively repaired (*V.C.H., Oxon.*, VI, 260).

[293] Under the influence of the Fermor family as lords of the manor, Somerton was one of the main centres of Catholicism in the county (see, *V.C.H., Oxon.*, VI, 300). 14 inhabitants were presented as recusants in 1666 and 10 in 1670 (MSS. Oxf. Dioc. c.9, f. 27^v; c.11, f. 14^v). 51 Papists in 1676; 31 excommunicated in 1680 (MS. Archd. pprs. Oxon. c. 121, f. 346). Fell listed 36 Papists in 1685 (MS. Oxf. Dioc. d.708, f. 151). 28 returned in 1706 (Hassall, p. 79). The rector considered that the numbers were decreasing by 1738 (*Secker Visitation*, p. 135).

[294] Another centre of Catholicism in the north-east of the county. 21 Papists in 1676; 15 listed by Fell in 1682 (MS. Oxf. Dioc. d.708, f. 152); 27 returned in 1706 (Hassall, p. 79); 9 in 1738 (*Secker Visitation*, p. 138).

[295] 3 Papists in 1676; one noted by Fell in 1682 (MS. Oxf. Dioc. d. 708, f. 139^v).

[296] In Sept. 1682, 45 men of Steeple Aston signed a petition to Fell complaining of their rector's neglect of parish affairs, to which the rector replied with his own complaints, which included many of the points noted here (MS. Oxf. Dioc. c.650, ff. 32–38).

[297] In Feb. 1684, probably as a result of Halton's findings at his visitation, the churchwardens appeared before the archdeacon's court, agreed to provide a sanctus bell, but said they could not proceed with repairs to the chapel until the bishop and archdeacon determined 'whose right it is to repair the same' (MS. Archd. pprs. Oxon. c.23, f. 65^v).

[298] See above, p. 62 and n. 217.

[299] See above, pp. 6–7.

[300] Excommunicated in 1684 (MS. Archd. pprs. Oxon. c.121, f. 28). He may be the same Henry Coleman who was licensed as a Presbyterian preacher in Tur Langton, Leics., in 1672 (Lyon Turner, II, 768).

[301] In Charlbury parish, see above, pp. 10–11.

[302] See above, p. 10.

[303] See above, p. 13.

[304] In Swalcliffe parish, see above, p. 62 and n. 221.

[305] Fell listed 2 dissenters and 2 absenters in 1685 (MS. Oxf. Dioc. d.708, f. 121^v).

[306] In Bloxham parish, see above, pp. 6–7.

[307] See above, p. 53, n. 68.

[308] Edward Herrell was called to the visitations of Easter and Michaelmas 1681 and Michaelmas 1682, and to Fell's triennial visitation in April 1682 (MSS. Oxf. Dioc. c.128, d.20).

[309] The minister of Swerford presented 10 parishioners and the churchwardens 19 as absent from the sacrament in 1666 (MS. Oxf. Dioc. c.9, ff. 113–14). 10 nonconformists in 1676. Fell

listed 3 Quakers in 1682 and 2 in 1685, but distinguished from them, 20 absenters from the sacrament (MS. Oxf. Dioc. d.708, ff. 124ᵛ, 125).

[310] See above, p. 34.

[311] The Quaker meeting at South Newington was one of the four preparative meetings of the Banbury Monthly Meeting. 8 Quakers (mistakenly listed as Popish recusants) were absent from their parish church, c.1663 (MS. Oxf. Dioc. c.430, f. 39); 5 of them were excommunicated in 1664 (MS. Oxf. Dioc. c.99, f. 242). 30 nonconformists in 1676. 7 inhabitants excommunicated in 1684 (MS. Archd. pprs. Oxon. c.121, f. 28ᵛ). The house of William Warner and Richard King was licensed as a meeting place in 1693 (Oldfield, VIII, 803). In 1738, there were about 17 Quakers, whose meeting house, 'licensed nearly 50 years ago', had a burial ground, 3 Presbyterian families and 2 Anabaptist families (*Secker Visitation*, p. 139).

[312] 6 'Seperatists' and 2 excommunicate Quakers listed, c.1663 (MS. Oxf. Dioc. c.430, f. 39). 43 nonconformists and 1 Papist in 1676. Fell listed 6 dissenters in 1685 (MS. Oxf. Dioc. d.708, f. 134). 7 inhabitants were excommunicated in 1684 (MS. Archd. pprs. Oxon. c.121, f. 28ᵛ), including Walter Coleman, to whose upkeep both Banbury and Witney monthly meetings of Quakers contributed in the 1680s (Witney Monthly Meeting minute book). In 1738, 20 Quakers in 6 families (*Secker Visitation*, p. 161).

[313] See above, p. 63 and n. 222.

[314] 1 nonconformist in 1676. Fell noted 1 Anabaptist and 1 Quaker in 1682 (MS. Oxf. Dioc. d.708, f. 75).

[315] 3 Papists in 1676. Fell listed 2 Papists in 1682 (MS. Oxf. Dioc. d.708, f. 81). 10 Papists returned in 1706 (Hassall, p. 80).

[316] 2 Papists in 1676. Fell listed 2 Papists in 1682 (MS. Oxf. Dioc. d.708, f. 79).

[317] 5 Popish recusants, c.1663 (MS. Oxf. Dioc. c.430, f.41). 6 Papists in 1676. 7 people presented by the churchwardens as absent from church, c.1680 (MS. Oxf. Dioc. b.68, f. 4). Fell listed 7 'dissenters', probably Papists, in 1682 and 11 in 1685 (MS. Oxf. Dioc. d.708, ff. 64ᵛ, 65). 6 Papists, plus children, in 1706 (Hassall, p. 79); none in 1738 (*Secker Visitation*, p. 113).

[318] 2 Papists and 4 nonconformists in 1676. 8 people presented by the churchwardens as absent from church, c.1680 (MS. Oxf. Dioc. b.68, f. 4). 2 Papists and 2 Quakers listed by Fell in 1682 (MS. Oxf. Dioc. d.708, f. 55ᵛ). 2 Papists and 1 Quaker, all old people, in 1738 (*Secker Visitation*, p. 114).

[319] 11 inhabitants, including 1 Papist, excommunicated for not attending church, 1662–64 (MS. Oxf. Dioc. c.99, ff. 238–44). 8 Papists and 7 nonconformists in 1676. 6 people presented by the churchwardens for not going to church, c.1680 (MS. Oxf. Dioc. b.68, f. 4ᵛ).

[320] 6 inhabitants listed as absent from church, c. 1663 (MS. Oxf. Dioc. c.430, f. 41ᵛ). 5 Papists in 1676. 7 Papists listed by Fell in 1682, and 23 'absenters' in 1685 (MS. Oxf. Dioc. d.708, ff. 55, 56).

[321] 33 nonconformists and 1 Papist in 1676. 3 people presented by the churchwardens as absent from church, c.1680; 2 of the same people listed by Fell in 1685 (MSS. Oxf. Dioc. b.68, f. 4; d.708, f. 59).

[322] 9 inhabitants, including 1 Papist, excommunicated, 1662–65 (MS. Oxf. Dioc. c.99, ff. 238–43). The house of Richard Titmarsh, licensed as a meeting place for the Anabaptists in 1672, was probably in the parish (Lyon Turner, II, 830). 3 Papists and 5 nonconformists in 1676. 3 dissenters listed by Fell in 1682 (MS. Oxf. Dioc. d.708, f. 60).

[323] 5 inhabitants excommunicated in 1662 for being absent from church (MS. Oxf. Dioc. c.99, f. 238). The house of Michael Mercer, licensed as a Congregational meeting place in 1672, was in the parish (Lyon Turner, II, 829). 4 nonconformists and 1 Papist in 1676. 8 people presented by the churchwardens for not going to church, c.1680 (MS. Oxf. Dioc. b. 68, f. 4ᵛ). The Quaker meeting house was built on land behind Silas Norton's house in St Giles in the parish, c.1687.

³²⁴ 9 inhabitants listed as absent from church, c.1663 (MS. Oxf. Dioc. c.430, f. 41). 10 nonconformists and 1 Papist in 1676. 6 Quakers presented by the churchwardens, c.1680, and 10 listed by Fell in 1682 and 1685 (MSS. Oxf. Dioc. b.68, f. 4; d.708, ff. 64, 63ᵛ).
³²⁵ 2 inhabitants excommunicated in 1662 (MS. Oxf. Dioc. c.99, f. 238).
³²⁶ James Beckford's house licensed as a Baptist meeting place in 1672 (Lyon Turner, II, 830). 8 nonconformists in 1676. 4 people presented by the churchwardens as absent from church, c. 1680; 4 dissenters listed by Fell in 1682 (MSS. Oxf. Dioc. b.68, f. 4ᵛ; d.708, f. 66).
³²⁷ 4 'absenters from sacraments' listed by Fell in 1682 (MS. Oxf. Dioc. d.708, f. 83).

APPENDIX

³²⁸ See above, p. 63 and n. 231.
³²⁹ Excommunicated in 1663 'for suffering private meetings in his house' (MS. Oxf. Dioc. c.99, f. 240ᵛ), and again in 1678 (MS. Archd. pprs. Oxon, c.121, f. 182).
³³⁰ Bishop Blandford saw a link between the parliamentary army of civil war times and dissenters here, and at Warborough, Chadlington, Hook Norton and Chadlington, see above, p. xiv.
³³¹ Probably William Farrington, who was ejected from the curacy of Elton, Herefs., in 1662 and was preaching in London between 1669 and 1683 (*Calamy Revised*, p. 191).
³³² Possibly Richard Mayo, c.1631–95, see *DNB*.
³³³ Thame was in the peculiar jurisdiction of the dean and chapter of Lincoln, not subject to the jurisdiction of the archdeacon of Oxford. The right of institution to the vicarage was disputed between the bishops of Lincoln and Oxford (*V.C.H., Oxon.*, VII, 201). The house of Edward Howes was licensed as a Congregational meeting place in 1672 (Lyon Turner, II, 829). 100 'utter dissenters', 32 of them Quakers, in 1676 (*V.C.H., Oxon.*, VII, 212). See *Oxon. Peculiars* for presentments of inhabitants of Thame for nonconformity in this period, especially p. 180, for a list of 70 who did not receive the sacrament or pay their dues and offerings to the vicar at Easter 1670. Applications were made for the licensing of the houses of Edward Howes and John Nott as meetings places in 1690, of John Nott and Samuel Horn in 1692, and of Stephen King in 1693 (Oldfield, VIII, 801, 802). In 1690, Nott had 'newly set up a constant meeting' (*Freedom after Ejection*, p. 85).
³³⁴ George Swinnock, see above, p. xvi.
³³⁵ Robert Bennet, see above, p. xvii.
³³⁶ Samuel Clarke, see above, p. xvii.
³³⁷ See above, p. 63 and n. 225.
³³⁸ See *V.C.H., Oxon.*, VIII, 245. He appeared before ecclesiastical courts in 1663 and 1668 and was excommunicated in 1669 (MSS. Oxf. Dioc. c.6, f. 63ᵛ; Archd. pprs. Oxon. c.17, f. 156; c.121, f. 379).
³³⁹ Excommunicated in 1664 for not paying the minister's dues (MS. Oxf. Dioc. c.99, f. 241ᵛ).
³⁴⁰ Excommunicated in 1664 for not paying the clerk's wages or the minister's dues (MS. Oxf. Dioc. c.99, f. 241ᵛ). Goods of his worth 9s. 6d. were distrained in April 1682, presumably in payment of a fine for not attending church (MS. D.D. Par. Watlington c.8, f. 32).
³⁴¹ See above, pp. 25–26.
³⁴² Appeared before ecclesiastical courts in 1664 and 1674, on both occasions admitted not attending his parish church and was admonished to do so (MSS. Oxf. Dioc. c.4, f. 218; Archd. pprs. Oxon. c.21, f. 86).
³⁴³ See above, p. 59 and n. 174.
³⁴⁴ With his wife, listed as a dissenter by Fell in 1682 (MS. Oxf. Dioc. d.708, f. 172).
³⁴⁵ Edward Huish of the Middle Temple bought an extensive farm in the parish (*V.C.H., Oxon.*, VIII, 101).

[346] Wormsley House, the home of Col. Adrian Scrope, was the meeting place for representatives of the Baptists of Henley, Reading and Abingdon in Oct. and Nov. 1652 (see E. A. Payne, *The Baptists of Berkshire*, London, 1951, pp. 11, 19).

[347] i.e., Kingston Blount in the parish of Aston Rowant, see above, pp. 2–5.

[348] Perhaps the Anabaptist, John Belcher of Haseley, who had preached against the restoration of Charles II in Oxford in 1660 (see *V.C.H., Oxon.*, VIII, 41).

[349] In the peculiar jurisdiction of the abbey of Dorchester, and exempt from the archdeacon's jurisdiction (*V.C.H., Oxon.*, VII, 53). For presentments of dissenters and the problems of the incumbent in this period, see *Oxon. Peculiars*, passim, especially pp. 91–92, 95.

[350] Mercer, regularly summoned before the ecclesiastical courts for keeping conventicles, 1667–80 (*Oxon. Peculiars*, pp. 85–95). He was imprisoned for 7 weeks in 1660 for refusing to take the oath of allegiance and all his goods were distrained in payment of a fine for meetings being held in his house in 1670 (Besse, *Sufferings*, I, 566, 572). He was one of the leading Quakers present at the quarterly meeting held in Oxford in 1676 (Witney Monthly Meeting minute book, 1675–1703).

[351] Presented as absent church and for keeping conventicles in 1667 and 1668 (*Oxon. Peculiars*, pp. 85, 86).

[352] Weaver, regularly summoned before the ecclesiastical courts for totally absenting himself from the church, keeping frequent conventicles, and denying the authority of the court (*Oxon. Peculiars*, pp. 86–87, 93–94).

[353] Regularly presented for being absent from church and keeping conventicles, 1672–86, excommunicated in 1681 (*Oxon. Peculiars*, pp. 147–51).

[354] 1632–1708. A prominent Baptist in Abingdon (see E. A. Payne, *The Baptists of Berkshire*, pp. 44, 60).

[355] Regular preacher to the Baptists of Abingdon, Longworth and Faringdon; imprisoned in Reading gaol with other active Baptists in 1660 (see E. A. Payne, *The Baptists of Berkshire*, pp. 39–40). Licensed to preach in the house of Katherine Peck in Abingdon in 1672 (Lyon Turner, II, 950).

[356] See above, p. 53 and n. 71.

[357] Excommunicated in 1664 for not going to church (MS. Oxf. Dioc. c.99, f. 242).

[358] John Dunce, ejected from the rectory of Hazleton, Gloucs., and in 1672 licensed to preach at Bourton on the Water (*Calamy Revised*, p. 172). Possibly the 'notorious Anabaptist' who was prevented from preaching in Cogges parish church in 1668 (MS. Archd. pprs. Oxon. c.119, f. 94^v).

[359] See above, p. 62 and n. 215.

[360] Josiah Diston, maltster. His house licensed as a Congregational meeting place in 1672 (Lyon Turner, II, 828). Often imprisoned for having meetings in his house (Thomas Crosby, *The History of the English Baptists*, London, 1739, II, 258). In his will, made in 1710 when he was 77 years old, Diston left 40s. *per annum* to John Thorley, the Baptist minister of Chipping Norton, and to his successor, and 40s. as 'church stock' (MS. Wills Oxon. 125/1/20).

[361] Probably Thomas Worden, the Congregationalist minister, who was active preaching in Gloucestershire, Berkshire, Warwickshire and Oxfordshire between 1669 and 1696 (*Freedom after Ejection*, p. 389).

[362] See above, p. 62 and n. 217.

[363] Maltster, excommunicated in 1665 and 1670 (MSS. Oxf. Dioc. c.99, f. 243^v; Archd. pprs. Oxon. c.121, f. 204). When 7 Baptist churches agreed at Moreton in Marsh in June 1655, to hold fellowship together for mutual comfort and edification, Wilmot signed the agreement for the Hook Norton church. He continued to attend these general meetings until they came to an abrupt end in 1660 (Joseph Ivimey, *History of the English Baptists*, London, 1814, II, 518). In his will, made in Jan. 1682, he left his house to his widow and the malthouse to his son Benjamin. His goods were valued for probate at £40 3s 6d (MS. Wills Oxon. 72/4/22).

[364] Excommunicated in 1665 for not attending church (MS. Oxf. Dioc. c.99, f. 244).

365 Excommunicated in 1663 for not attending church (MS. Oxf. Dioc. c.99, f. 243^v). Burial recorded in the Quaker register in Feb. 1680 (O.R.O., BMM III/5).
366 i.e., Milton under Wychwood, see above, p. 53, n. 68.
367 In 1660 imprisoned for 7 weeks and his goods distrained after the Quaker meeting at Milton was broken up by the justices. In 1662 one of 12 Quakers fined £5 for unlawful assembly (Besse, *Sufferings*, I, 567, 568). He may be the Robert Seacole, shepherd, whose will and inventory of 1707 survive (MS. Wills Oxon. 63/1/29).
368 See above, pp. 1–2.
369 See above, p. 48 and n. 1.
370 Joyce Swift was buried in the Quaker burial ground in Adderbury in Aug. 1698 (O.R.O., BMM III/5). Her will and inventory survive (MS. Wills Oxon. 150/1/33).
371 Samuel Wells, see above, p. xv.
372 Thomas Whately, see above, p. 48 and n. 4.
373 Christopher Newell; B.A., Magdalen Hall Oxford, 1655; ejected from Bloxham, 1662; buried at Adwell, 1670.
374 20 nonconformists in 1676. 8 Quaker families throughout this period, who seem to have attended the meeting at Shutford (*V.C.H., Oxon.*, IX, 158).
375 Ejected from his cottage in Broughton, c.1655, he moved to Tadmarton; imprisoned for 25 weeks in 1658 for attending a Quaker meeting; his family regularly had goods distrained for non-payment of tithes, 1673–1706 (*V.C.H., Oxon.*, IX, 158). Buried in the Quaker burial ground in Banbury in June 1703 (O.R.O., BMM III/5). Probably the yeoman whose will was proved in 1704 (MS. Wills Oxon. 53/2/9).
376 With Benjamin Ward, excommunicated in 1663 for refusing to pay a church rate (MSS. Oxf. Dioc. c.6, f. 7^v; c.99, f. 239^v). Buried in the Quaker burial ground in Banbury in Dec. 1700 (O.R.O., BMM III/5). In his will described as yeoman, he left lands in Drayton and Hook Norton; his goods valued for probate at £204 5s. (MS. Wills Oxon. 28/1/37).
377 Excommunicated in 1663 (see above, n. 376). Imprisoned several times during the 1660s and sheep worth £20 distrained in 1672 (*V.C.H., Oxon.*, IX, 158). Buried in the Quaker burial ground in South Newington in 1695 (O.R.O., BMM III/5).
378 See above, p. 62 and n. 221.
379 Fell noted in his diocese book in 1682 that Archer was the teacher of the Anabaptists and that they met in his house, which by 1685 had passed into the possession of a shepherd, Richard Gilkes (MS. Oxf. Dioc. d.708, ff. 133, 132^v). In the transactions of the Baptist general assemblies in London, 1689–92, Charles Archer was named as the pastor and representative of the church at Hook Norton (Joseph Ivimey, *History of the English Baptists*, London, 1814, II, 519).
380 Probably James or Samuel Wilmot, see above, notes 363, 364.
381 The register of the Sibford meeting of Quakers records the burial of Thomas Gilkes 'worthy of memory' in June 1699 (O.R.O., BMM III/1).
382 See above, pp. 6–7.
383 Thomas and Ann Ingram were excommunicated in 1663 for having conventicles in their house (MS. Oxf. Dioc. c.99, f. 240^v). His goods were valued for probate at £9 19s 6d in 1672, when he was described as a husbandman (MS. Wills Oxon. 82/1/19).
384 George Aston was excommunicated in 1664, 1665 and 1684 (MSS. Oxf. Dioc. c.99, ff. 241, 243; Archd. pprs. Oxon. c.121, f. 28). Goods worth £20 were taken in payment of fines for attending meetings in the 1660s (Besse, *Sufferings*, I, 572). Probably died in 1691 (MS. Wills Oxon. 76/2/13).
385 i.e., Bicester. An active conventicle developed here with John Troughton then Henry Cornish as its ministers. 2 inhabitants were excommunicated in 1664 as dissenters who endeavoured to persuade others (MS. Oxf. Dioc. c.99, ff. 241^v, 242). 15 people were presented as absent church in 1668 (MS. Archd. pprs. Oxon. c.17, ff. 96–97). John Troughton's house was licensed as a Presbyterian meeting place in 1672 and Henry Cornish's in 1691

(Lyon Turner, II, 827; Oldfield, VIII, 801). In 1728 a licence was sought for a new meeting house in Water Lane, adjoining the Swan Inn, recently built to replace the 'old one now ruinous' (Oldfield, VIII, 806). In 1738 the vicar reported 'several hundred' Presbyterians, with a large meeting house, and 6 families of Quakers, with a meeting house (*Secker Visitation*, p. 30). The earliest reference to Quakers here is in 1676. In 1678 the Witney quarterly meeting gave permission for monthly meetings to be held here. By 1816, the meeting had lapsed, though the meeting house still stood in a yard off Sheep Street (*V.C.H., Oxon.*, VI, 50).

[386] In 1667 and 1668 presented for not attending church or receiving Holy Communion, excommunicated in 1670 (MSS. Archd. pprs. Oxon. c.17, ff. 18, 96^v, 126; c.121, f. 37).

[387] Edward Bagshaw, see above, p. xvii.

[388] Samuel Wells, see above, p. xv.

[389] George Swinnock, see above, p. xvi.

[390] John Dod, fellow of Corpus Christi College, Oxford, 1648; ejected from the rectory of Lower Heyford in 1662; settled in Witney (*Calamy Revised*, p. 165).

[391] John Troughton, see above, p. xv.

[392] Thomas Whately, see above, p. 48 and n. 4.

[393] Thomas Lamplugh, incumbent of Charlton on Otmoor, wrote to Sir Joseph Williamson in Jan. 1669 of the boldness of the dissenters in the area, who had 'set apart a house at Bicester for a public meeting place, and made a pulpit in it'. He added that unless the conventicle was suppressed 'they will grow so numerous that I dread the result' (*Cal. S.P. Dom.* 1668/9, p. 151).

[394] See above, p. 55 and n. 111.

[395] His house was licensed as a Presbyterian meeting place in 1672 (Lyon Turner, II, 827). He was probably the mercer whose goods, when he died in 1684, were valued for probate at £431 2s 3½d (MS. Wills Oxon. 77/2/25).

[396] Widow of James Wyer, vicar of Deddington during the Commonwealth (H. M. Colvin, *A History of Deddington*, London, 1963, p. 97).

[397] See above, p. 48 and n. 4.

[398] See above, p. 65 and n. 262.

[399] The death of his father, the vicar of Brize Norton, in 1663, was seen by the Quakers as the result of having to read in public the sentence of excommunication on his own son (Besse, *Sufferings*, I, 568). Dring was among the 21 Quakers sent to Oxford gaol in 1660 after meetings in Milton under Wychwood and Brize Norton were broken up; fined for unlawful assembly in 1662; excommunicated in 1663 'for saying his conscience would not permit him to go to the parish church and that he is a church himself (MSS. Oxf. Dioc. c.99, f. 239; c.4, f. 72^v). One of the 26 leading Quakers who attended the quarterly meeting in Oxford in April 1676 (Witney Monthly Meeting minute book, 1675–1703). In 1689 he gave up his position as trustee of the Milton meeting house to a younger man.

[400] Only 5 nonconformists in 1676. Edward Franklyn of the parish was presented as a Quaker in 1670 (MS. Oxf. Dioc. c.11, f. 5). Fell listed 5 dissenters in 1682 (MS. Oxf. Dioc. d.708, f. 111^v). 2 families of Quakers in 1738 (*Secker Visitation*, p. 109).

[401] Imprisoned for non-payment of tithes in 1659 (Besse, *Sufferings*, I, 566). Excommunicated in 1670 and charged with being absent from church and not paying a church rate in 1674 (MSS. Archd. pprs. Oxon. c.121, f. 250; c.22, f. 183). Buried in the Quaker burial ground in Sibford in June 1688 (O.R.O., BMM. III/5).

[402] In North Leigh parish, see above, n. 400.

[403] Dissent in Cogges was no doubt encouraged by its proximity to Witney (see above, p. 61 and n. 211), and by a vacancy in the living. When the minister, John Parkinson died in Feb. 1668, he was not immediately replaced. This gave Richard Crutchfield (see below, n. 406) the opportunity to invite nonconformist ministers to preach in the parish church (MS. Archd. pprs. Oxon. c.119, f. 90). Fell listed 2 Quakers and 1 Anabaptist in 1682, 1 Quaker in 1685 (MS. Oxf. Dioc. d.708, ff. 95, 94^v).

[404] Francis Blake, woollen draper of London, had, with his son William, a merchant, bought the manor of Cogges in 1667. Neither appears to have continued this encouragement of dissent. Francis died in 1693 and his son in 1695, when the latter left numerous benefactions to Witney and Cogges, including a supplement to the income of the incumbent of Cogges, on condition that he catechised the children of the parish regularly.

[405] In March 1669 he was charged with having conventicles in his house, with inviting nonconformist ministers to preach in the parish church and with not receiving the sacrament. He admitted having several meetings in his house 'by permission and leave of . . . Mr. Blake', whose bailiff he was. When he did not appear before the bishop's court in Nov. to present proof of having received the sacrament, he was excommunicated (MS. Oxf. Dioc. c.9, ff. 210^v, 228).

[406] In July 1669 he was accused of allowing nonconformists to preach in the parish church and of speaking against the clergy of the established church. Thomas Gregory gave evidence that in 1668 he had accompanied his brother, Dr Francis Gregory of Witney, who sometimes supplied the cure at Cogges, to prevent a 'notorious Anabaptist' from preaching there. He gave an account of the verbal exchange between Crutchfield and Dr Gregory, during which Crutchfield had said that 'the clergy of England were none of Christ's ministers', and had spoken against the civil magistrates. He had concluded by leading a large part of the congregation out of the parish church, saying 'Come, the word of God is as good in a house as in the Church' (MS. Archd. pprs. Oxon. c.119, ff. 95–97^v, 109^v–10, 125–28).

[407] See above, p. xvi.

[408] Henry Cornish, see above, p. xvi.

[409] See above, n. 390.

[410] See above, p. xv.

[411] William Conway, matriculated at Magdalen Hall, Oxford, 1658; lived at Witney; in 1672 licensed to preach in Malmesbury, where he was still active as a Prebyterian minister in 1690 (*Freedom after Ejection*, p. 242).

INDEX OF PERSONS

Aldrich, Henry, Dean of Christ Church, xiii
Allen, Ann, of Enstone, 16
Allen, Samuel, of Enstone, 16
Allestree, Richard, Canon of Christ Church, xi
Allnutt, Sir Henry, of Ibstone House, Bucks., xxvi, xxxviii, 22 (3), 23, 26, 58 (n 153)
Ambrose, Francis, of Wilcote, 46, 47
Anker, William, of South Leigh, 61 (n 210)
Anne family, of North Aston, 62 (n 213)
Appletree, John, of Deddington, 55 (n 103)
Appletree, Philip, of Deddington, 55 (n 111)
Archer, Charles, of Burdrop, 44, 45, 71 (n 379)
Ashfield, Thomas, rector of Combe and Stonesfield, 12, 13, 54 (n 93)
Ashwell, George, rector of Hanwell, xxxii, xxxvi, 14, 20, 57 (ns 136–37)
Ason. *See* Aston
Aston, George, of Bloxham, 44, 71 (n 384)
Atkins, Catherine, of Ibstone, Bucks., 23, 58 (n 154)
Atkins, William, of Thame, 40
Atkyns, Robert, of Stow on the Wold, Gloucs., xxix
Austin, Elizabeth, of Islip, 34, 36, 64 (n 239)

Badger, Mrs, of Oxford (St Giles), 39
Bagshaw, Edward, nonconformist minister, xvii–xviii, 47
Ball, Joseph, of Bloxham, xxvi
Barfoot, Thomas, of South Leigh, 38, 61 (n 210), 66 (n 280)
Barford. *See* Barfoot
Baritt, Isabell, of Rousham, 59 (n 183)
Bartlett, Dorothy, of Bampton, 5, 51 (n 34)
Bartlett, Edmund, of Bampton, 51 (n 34)
Bartlett, Elizabeth, of Lew, 51 (n 34)
Bartlett, John, of Bampton, 51 (n 34)
Bartlett, Mary, of Bampton, 5, 51 (n 34)
Bates, Jeremiah, vicar of Black Bourton, 6, 51 (n 44)
Bayly, John, rector of Fringford, xxxvi, 17, 56 (n 127)
Beau, William, Bishop of Llandaff, 6, 48 (n 6), 51 (n 46)
Beckford, James, of Wolvercote, 69 (n 326)
Beckingham, John, vicar of Enstone, xxxvi, 17, 34, 56 (n 126)
Beckingham, William, of Charlbury, 56 (n 126)
Beesly, John, of Warborough, 42, 43, 70 (n 352)
Belcher, John, of Haseley, 43, 70 (n 348)
Bennet, Robert, nonconformist minister, xvii, xviii, 41
Bennet, Thomas, of Aston Rowant, 4, 49 (ns 17, 19)
Bennett, Elizabeth, of Hethe, 57 (n 143)
Bennett, Henry, of Hethe, 57 (n 143)
Berrey, Edward, of Caversham, 8
Bertie, Capt. Henry, xxvi, 5, 49 (n 20)

INDEX OF PERSONS

Bettres, Edward, of Weald, 5, 50 (n 25)
Bicknell. *See* Bignell
Bigg, John, of Swyncombe, 35, 36
Bignell, John, of Deddington, 14, 55 (n 103), 56 (n 122)
Bignell, Timothy, of Deddington, 46, 55 (ns 103, 111), 56 (n 122), 72 (n 395)
Bill, Thomas, rector of Over Worton, 32, 61 (n 203)
Binfield, Henry, of Caversham, 9
Binham, John, of Chalgrove, 7, 52 (n 54)
Birch, Samuel, vicar of Bampton, xxiii, 50 (n 24)
Blackhall, Richard, of Caversham, 8
Blake, Francis, of Cogges, xv, 46, 47 (2), 73 (ns 404–5)
Blake, William, of Cogges, 73 (n 404)
Blandford, Walter, Bishop of Oxford, xiv, xv, xxiii, xxvi, xxxv (n 127), 19, 23, 58 (n 155), 69 (n 330)
Blount, Charles, of Mapledurham, 8, 52 (n 58)
Blount, Elizabeth, of Mapledurham, 8, 52 (ns 57–59)
Blount, Lyster, of Mapledurham, 52 (n 57)
Blount, Walter, of Mapledurham, 52 (n 57)
Blount, William, of Mapledurham, 52 (ns 57–58)
Boham, Hugh, rector of Harpsden, xxxvii, 21, 57 (n 139), 58 (n 149)
Bolt, Mary, of Islip, 58 (n 164)
Brice, John, nonconformist minister, 41
Brickland, Catherine, of Aston, 5, 51 (n 36)
Brickland, Mark, of Aston, 51 (n 36)
Brigham, Anthony, of Caversham, 8
Brigham, Thomas, of Caversham, 8
Brooke family, of North Aston, 62 (n 213)
Brooks, Joshua, of Burford, xxxiv, 35, 64 (n 233)
Brooks, Richard, of Charlbury, 10, 53 (n 81)
Browne family, of Kiddington, 62 (n 212)
Bullock, Ann, of South Leigh, 66 (n 280)
Burnard, Alexander, of Henley, 63 (n 231)
Burnard, William, of Caversfield, xv
Burnet, Gilbert, Bishop of Salisbury, xiv
Burnet, William, nonconformist minister, 56 (n 121)
Burton, John, of Thame, 40
Busby, Edward, of Radford, 16 (2), 34, 56 (n 124)
Busby, Grace, of Charlbury, 10, 53 (n 73)
Busby, Thomas, of Charlbury, 10, 53 (n 73)
Bush, Edward, of Harpsden, 57 (n 140)
Bushell, John, vicar of Lewknor, xxxix (2), 26, 59 (n 177)
Butler, James, 1st Duke of Ormonde, xii
Butler, James, 2nd Duke of Ormonde, xii
Butler, John, of Caversham, 9
Button, Mr, 43

Cadogan, William, 1st Earl Cadogan, 52 (n 62)
Calamy, Edmund, xv, xvi
Callow, Benjamin, rector of Stow on the Wold, Gloucs., xxix
Carpenter, John, of Bampton, 5, 51 (n 35)
Carpenter, John, of Witney, 61 (n 211)
Carpenter, Richard, of Charlbury, 10, 53 (ns 77–78)
Cartwright, Thomas, of Caversham, 8
Cary, Henry, 4th Viscount Falkland, xxv

INDEX OF PERSONS

Castle, James, of Duns Tew, 56 (n 117)
Castle, Thomas, of Caversham, 8
Charles I, 56 (n 127)
Charles II, xvii, xxi, 6, 70 (n 348)
Charnelhouse, Alexander, rector of Salford, xxxix (n 158), 29, 59 (n 187)
Chessus, Joan, of Clanfield, 51 (n 43)
Chitch, John, senior, of Kingston Blount, 4 (2), 5, 49 (n 15)
Chitch, John, junior, of Kingston Blount, 4, 49 (ns 18–19)
Chitch, Lucy, of Kingston Blount, 49 (n 19)
Chitch, Richard, of Kingston Blount, 2, 3 (2), 5, 42, 43, 49 (ns 10, 14, 16–17, 19)
Churchill, Thomas, of Sarsden, 29, 60 (n 188)
Clanfield, Francis, of Clifton, 55 (n 111)
Clare, Richard, of Charlbury, 10, 53 (ns 77–78)
Clarendon, Earl of. *See* Hyde
Clark, Mary, 62 (n 215)
Clarke, Samuel, nonconformist minister, xvii, xviii, 41
Clavering, Robert, Bishop of Llandaff, xiii
Clement, Robert, of Chadlington, 42, 43, 70 (n 357)
Clerke, John, of Aston Rowant, xxxviii (2), 2 (2), 3, 49 (n 9)
Clifton, Alice, of Wigginton, 63 (n 222)
Clinch, —, of Bampton, 5
Cole, Leonard, of Caversham, 8
Cole, Thomas, nonconformist minister, 63 (n 231)
Coleman, Henry, of Bloxham, 39, 67 (n 300)
Coleman, Walter, of Great Tew, 68 (n 312)
Coles, Mrs, of Bampton, 5
Coles, Edward, of Bletchingdon, 53 (n 70)
Coles, William, vicar of Charlbury, 10, 53 (n 70)
Colier, Mrs, of Witney, 61 (n 211)
Collier, Nathaniel, vicar of Duns Tew, xxxvi, 15, 56 (n 119)
Collins, Mr, 41
Collis, Edward, of Caversham, 9
Combes, John, of Abingdon, Berks., 43, 47, 70 (n 355)
Compton, Henry, Bishop of London, xxxv (n 127)
Connoway. *See* Conway
Conway, William, nonconformist minister, 47, 73 (n 411)
Cook, Hannah, of Ibstone, Bucks., 23, 58 (n 154)
Cook, Thomas, of Ibstone, Bucks., 23, 58 (n 154)
Cooper, Anthony Ashley, 1st Earl of Shaftesbury, 54 (n 88)
Cooper, Richard, of Aston Rowant, 4, 5, 49 (ns 14, 19)
Cope, Sir Anthony, of Hanwell, 57 (ns 136–37)
Coppe, Abiezer, 19, 56 (n 135)
Cornish, Henry, nonconformist minister, xvi, xviii (2), xxiii, 47, 66 (n 277), 71 (n 385)
Cornish, William, of Henley, 63 (n 231)
Corpson, Mr, xxvii
Coven, Stephen, nonconformist minister, 7, 52 (n 53), 65 (n 255)
Cox, John, of Heythrop, 60 (n 195)
Cox, Josiah, of Adderbury, 48 (n 3)
Cox, Samuel, of Milton, 48 (n 3)
Coxon, Henry, curate of Great Tew, 34, 35, 63 (n 223)
Crace, William, of London, 40
Crasse, Thomas, of Finstock, 54 (n 83)
Crewe, Nathaniel, Bishop of Durham, xxxv (n 127)
Crips, John, of Bampton, 5, 50 (n 32)

INDEX OF PERSONS

Cromwell, Oliver, Lord Protector, xiv, 45
Cromwell, Richard, Lord Protector, xiii
Crook, Christopher, of Aston Rowant, 4, 5, 49 (ns 15–16)
Crutchfield, Richard, of Cogges, 47, 72 (n 403), 73 (n 406)
Curtice, Capt. Thomas, of Caversham, 8, 52 (n 61)
Curtice, William, of Caversham, 8
Cutler, John, of Henley, 64 (n 231)
Cyprian, St, xxxi, xxxii (3), 18, 23

Dagley, Jane, of Hethe, 21, 57 (n 146)
Dagley, John, of Hethe, 21
Davies, Nehemiah, rector of Mongewell, 27, 59 (n 180)
Davis, Joseph, of Chipping Norton, xxiv
Dawes, Abraham, of Duns Tew, 15, 56 (n 118)
Day, Richard, of Lower Heyford, 63 (n 225)
Dean, Richard, of Caversham, 8
Delaval, Sir Ralph, 52 (n 59)
Delaval, Robert, 8, 52 (n 59)
Diston, Josiah, of Chipping Norton, xxiv–xxv, 42, 62 (n 215), 70 (n 360)
Dod, John, nonconformist minister, 47 (2), 72 (n 390)
Dolben, John, Canon of Christ Church, xi
Dolly, Robert, of Rousham, 27–28, 59 (ns 183, 185)
Dormer, Robert, of Rousham, 27, 28, 59 (ns 182–84)
Downer, Anne, of Charlbury, 53 (n 71)
Doyley, Cope, curate of Hook Norton, 62 (n 217)
Doyly, Bray, of Adderbury, xv, xxxiv, xxxviii, 1, 34, 44, 48 (ns 1–2)
Drelincourt, Peter, xii
Dring, Francis, of Brize Norton, 46, 47 (2), 65 (n 262), 72 (n 399)
Drinkwater, William, of Gagingwell, 51 (n 42)
Drye, Abraham, nonconformist minister, 61 (n 207)
Dunce, John, nonconformist minister, 43, 70 (n 358)
Dutton, Ellis, rector of Rousham, 59 (n 184)
Dutton, Richard, rector of Rousham, 28, 59 (n 184)

East, Mary, of Watlington, 40, 69 (n 339)
Edwards, Jonathan, rector of Kiddington, 35, 64 (n 234)
Edwin, Elizabeth, of Henley, 37
Evans, Richard, rector of Hethe, xxxi, xxxvii, xxxix, 22, 58 (n 150)
Evans, Robert, of Aston, 5, 51 (n 39)
Evelyn, John, xi
Everard, Samuel, rector of Swyncombe, 36, 64 (n 241)
Everett. *See* Everard

Fairfax, Thomas, 3rd Baron Fairfax, 56 (n 127)
Falkland, Viscount. *See* Cary
Fardon, John, of Deddington, 55 (n 111)
Fardon, Thomas, of Deddington, 55 (n 111)
Farmer, —, of Bampton, 5
Farren, James, nonconformist minister, 59 (n 179)
Farrington, William, nonconformist minister, 41, 69 (n 331)
Feild, Edward, of Bampton, 5, 51 (n 40)
Fell, John, Bishop of Oxford,
　as Bishop, xiii–xiv, xxx–xxxi, xxxiii
　as Dean of Christ Church, xi–xii, xiii (2)

as a Royalist, xi, xiii
as Vice-Chancellor, xii
attitude to clergy, xxviii–xxix, xxxv
attitude to dissenters, xxvii
diocese book, xxxiii–xxxiv, 48–73 *passim*
letters to him, xix, xxix, xxxi–xxxiii, xxxvi–xxxix, 1–32
queries to Archdeacon Halton, 33–36
translation of St Cyprian's tract, xxxi–xxxii, 18, 23
Fermor, Richard, of Tusmore, 36, 57 (n 141), 64 (n 238)
Fermor family, of Tusmore, xxxviii, 21, 57 (n 141), 58 (n 151), 67 (ns 288, 293)
Fettiplace family, of Swyncombe, 65 (n 253)
Fiennes, William, 1st Viscount Saye and Sele, xxv, 48 (n 1)
Fitzgerald, John, 18th Earl of Kildare, 8, 52 (n 62)
Fletcher, Thomas, of Middle Barton, xxiii (n 65)
Fletcher family, of Steeple Barton, 66 (n 281)
Ford, John, 34, 36, 63 (n 230)
Ford, Stephen, nonconformist minister, xxiii, 62 (n 215)
Forster, Roger, of Caversham, 8, 9
Franklyn, Edward, of North Leigh, 72 (n 400)
Froyser, Jeremy, nonconformist minister, 64 (n 231)
Fruen, Edward, of Caversham, 9
Fruen, John, of Caversham, 9

Ganner, Mary, 12, 54 (n 96)
Ganner, Richard, 12
Gardner, William, of Adderbury, 44
Gilbert, Thomas, nonconformist minister, xvi
Gilbert, William, nonconformist minister, 61 (n 211), 66 (n 277)
Giles, Thomas, of Wigginton, 63 (n 222)
Gilkes, —, of Drayton, 14
Gilkes, Richard, of Burdrop, 71 (n 379)
Gilkes, Thomas, of Sibford Gower, 44, 71 (n 381)
Gill, John, of Hethe, 21, 57 (n 143)
Gill, Margaret, of Hethe, 21, 57 (n 143)
Gillingham, John, of Henley, 37
Gilpin, Thomas, of Warborough, xxiii, 42, 43, 70 (n 350)
Gom, Mary, of Chinnor, 11, 54 (n 86)
Gom, Richard, of Chinnor, 11, 54 (n 86)
Gower, John, of Weald, xxiv
Grant, Thomas, of Charlbury, 10, 53 (n 81)
Green, Mrs, of Bampton, 5
Green, Alice, of South Weston, 60 (n 197)
Greenaway, John, of Burford, 35
Greenwood family, of Chastleton, 54 (n 85)
Gregory, Christian, of Pyrton, 64 (n 251)
Gregory, Dr Francis, of Witney, 73 (n 406)
Gregory, Giles, of Caversham, xxvi (2), 5, 8, 26, 49 (n 21)
Gregory, Henry, rector of Middleton Stoney, xxxi, 27, 59 (n 178)
Gregory, Thomas, 73 (n 406)
Gregory, William, of Pyrton, 64 (n 251)
Grendown, John, of Watlington, 37, 64 (n 242), 65 (n 256)
Gun, John, 45, 71 (n 376)
Gunn, John, of Clanfield, xxiv

INDEX OF PERSONS

Hadduck, Thomas, xxiii
Haines, Richard, of Burford, 35
Haiward, Richard, of Harpsden, 57 (n 138)
Hakins, Mary, of Watlington, 37
Hall, Christopher, of Caversham, 8
Halton, Timothy, Archdeacon of Oxford, xxxiv (4), xxxix, xl, 33–39
Hamblen, Michael, of Caversham, 8
Hammond, Henry, Canon of Christ Church, xxvii
Hampden, Richard, xvi
Harcourt, Sir Philip, xvi, 66 (n 277)
Harley, Edward, 2nd Earl of Oxford, xiii
Harper, John, of Watlington, 65 (n 255)
Harris, —, of Bampton, 5
Harris, Alexander, of Charlbury, 10, 42, 53 (n 72)
Harris, Anthony, of Deddington, 55 (n 111)
Harris, John, of Charlbury, 10, 53 (n 81)
Harris, Joshua, of Brize Norton, 65 (n 262)
Harris, Mary, wife of Alexander, of Charlbury, 10, 53 (n 72)
Harris, Mary, wife of John, of Charlbury, 10, 53 (n 81)
Harris, Richard, of Shorthampton, 11, 54 (n 82)
Harris, Thomas, of Bicester, 46, 72 (n 386)
Harvie, Mary, of Hethe, 21
Harwood, William, of Hook Norton, 62 (n 217)
Hawkes, John, of Islip, 58 (n 164)
Hawkins, Robert, curate of Beckley, xxviii
Hawze, Mrs, of Chilson, 10
Herald. *See* Herrell
Heron. *See* Herrell
Herrell, Edward, of Salford, 39, 64 (n 242), 67 (n 308)
Higgins, John, of Over Worton, 60 (n 202)
Hill, —, of Bampton, 5
Hill, John, of Bampton, 5, 50 (n 30)
Hill, William, of Caversham, 8
Hinton, Margaret, of Warborough, 42 (2), 70 (n 351)
Holloway, John, rector of Chastleton, 11, 54 (n 84)
Hollyman, Elizabeth, 60 (n 198)
Hollyman, Richard, miller, 49 (n 21), 60 (n 198), 64 (n 244)
Hookes, Ellis, 60 (n 189)
Horn, Samuel, of Thame, 69 (n 333)
Hough, John, vicar of North Aston, 64 (n 235)
Howes, Edward, of Thame, 69 (n 333)
Hubbard, Francis, nonconformist minister, xxiii, 61 (n 211)
Huish, Edward, of Lewknor, 40, 69 (n 345)
Hunt, Hugh, of Kingston Blount, 3 (2), 49 (n 11)
Hurst, Alice, of Combe, 12–13, 54 (n 97)
Hyde, Edward, 1st Earl of Clarendon, xii (n 6)

Ingram, Ann, of Bloxham, 71 (n 383)
Ingram, Thomas, of Bloxham, 44, 71 (n 383)

James II, xxx, xl
Jay, Charles, rector of Chinnor, 54 (n 88)
Jay, Stephen, rector of Chinnor, 11, 54 (n 88)
Jennings, Edward, curate of Hook Norton, xxviii, 62 (n 217)

INDEX OF PERSONS

Jennings, Edward, of Oxford (St Michael), xxii (n 55)
Jones family, of Chastleton, 54 (n 85)
Justice, Ann, of Hethe, 21, 57 (n 142)
Justice, Edward, of Hethe, 21
Justice, John, of Caversham, 8, 9

Kennett, White, Bishop of Peterborough, xvi (n 29)
Kerie, John, rector of Cornwell, xxxix, 13, 39, 54 (n 99)
Kildare, Earl of. *See* Fitzgerald
King, Richard, of Chinnor, 54 (n 89)
King, Richard, of South Newington, 68 (n 311)
King, Stephen, of Thame, 69 (n 333)
Kite, John, of Salford, 59 (n 187)

Lambert, John, xiv, 45
Lamley, John, of Hook Norton, 45, 71 (n 365)
Lamplugh, Thomas, 72 (n 393)
Langford, Thomas, of Charlbury, xxii (n 55)
Langley, Henry, nonconformist minister, xvi, xviii, 47
Laughton, Alice, 12, 54 (n 96)
Lee, Sir Francis Henry, of Quarrendon and Ditchley, xv (n 16)
Lely, Sir Peter, xi
Lewinton, Sarah, of Pyrton, 65 (n 251)
Lloyd, William, Bishop of Peterborough, xxxvii (2), xxxviii
Lord, Laurence, of Cottisford, 36 (3), 64 (n 237)
Lort. *See* Lord
Lovejoy, Henry, of Caversham, 9
Lovejoy, William, of Caversham, 8
Low, John, of Chalgrove, 7
Luggrove, William, 43, 70 (n 353)

Mady, James, of Burford, 33, 35
Makepeace, Mary, of Deddington, 55 (n 106)
Makepeace, Thomas, of Deddington, 14
Manning, Richard, vicar of Chalgrove, xxxvi, 7, 52 (n 55)
Marsh, Deborah, of Lower Heyford, 63 (n 225)
Marsh, John, of Lower Heyford, 34, 36, 63 (n 225)
Marsh, Rebecca, of Lower Heyford, 63 (n 225)
Mather, Samuel, of Witney, 62 (n 211)
May, —, of Bampton, 5
Maynard, Richard, of Clifton, 55 (n 111)
Mayo, Richard, nonconformist minister, 41, 69 (n 332)
Mercer, Michael, of Oxford (St Mary Magdalen), 68 (n 323)
Miles, Elizabeth, of Charlbury, 10, 53 (n 79)
Miles, John, of Charlbury, 53 (n 79)
Millers, Elizabeth, of Drayton, 14, 55 (n 113)
Millers, William, of Drayton, 14, 55 (n 113)
Minchin, Thomas, of Burford, xxii (n 56), xxiii, 32, 61 (n 208)
Mins, Thomas, of Begbroke, 37
Monday, John, of Aston Rowant, xxxviii, 2
Monk, Joan, 51 (n 43)
Monk, John, of Black Bourton, 6, 51 (n 43)
Monk, Thomas, of Filkins, 6, 51 (n 43), 58 (n 166)
Monmouth, Duke of. *See* Scott

INDEX OF PERSONS

Moore, Brian, rector of Hardwick, 34, 36, 63 (n 227)
Moreton, Sir William, xxv
Morris, Elizabeth, 12, 54 (n 96)
Morris, Richard, 12
Morton, Adam, rector of Drayton, xxxvii, 15, 55 (n 115)

Nash, Nathaniel, of Watlington, 65 (n 255)
Newell, Christopher, nonconformist minister, 45, 71 (n 373)
Newton, Emanuel, of Hethe, 21
Newton, Margaret, of Hethe, 21, 57 (n 144)
Nibb, Elizabeth, of Wigginton, 63 (n 222)
Nichols, John, of Islip, 34, 36, 64 (n 239)
Nichols, Thomas, of Shutford, 63 (n 221)
North, Christopher, of Lewknor, 40, 69 (n 344)
North, Elizabeth, of Aston Rowant, 49 (n 16)
North, Elizabeth, of Lewknor, 26, 59 (ns 173–74)
North, John, senior, of Aston Rowant, 4, 42, 43, 49 (ns 16, 22)
North, John, junior, of Aston Rowant, 4, 49 (ns 16–17)
North, Mary, of Kingston Blount, 42
North, William, of Lewknor, 26, 40, 59 (ns 173–74)
Norton, Silas, of Oxford (St Giles), 68 (n 323)
Nott, John, of Thame, 69 (n 333)

Oak, Mrs, of Bampton, 5, 51 (n 38)
Oldisworth, James, rector of Kencot, 25, 59 (n 168)
Oovey. *See* Ovey
Ordoway, Philip, of Deddington, 13–14, 55 (ns 102, 111)
Ormonde, Duke of. *See* Butler
Overbury, Sir Thomas, xxxix
Overy, Lawrence, of Dorchester, xxi (n 52)
Ovey, John, of Watlington, 40, 41, 69 (n 338)
Ovey, Thomas, of Watlington, 65 (n 255)
Owen, Katherine, of Hempton, 14, 55 (n 107)
Owen, Thomas, of Hempton, 14 (2), 55 (n 107)
Oxford, Earl of. *See* Harley

Pace, John, of Caversham, 8
Pack, Samuel, of Burford, xxxiv (3), 32, 35, 61 (n 206)
Packford, Thomas, of Finstock, 54 (n 83)
Page, Nicholas, curate of Bloxham, xxxvi, 7, 51 (n 48)
Palmer, John, Archdeacon of Northampton, xix
Parish, Timothy, of Charlbury, 10, 53 (n 78)
Parkinson, John, minister of Cogges, 72 (n 403)
Parr, Richard, curate of Ibstone, xxxii (2), 24, 58 (ns 157, 162)
Parsons, Robert, curate of Adderbury, xxxiii, 2, 6, 35, 48 (n 6), 51 (n 47)
Paul, William, Bishop of Oxford, xxii, xxxv (n 127), 11, 54 (n 87)
Payne, John, of Fringford, 18, 56 (n 130)
Pears, —, of Bampton, 5
Peck, Katherine, of Abingdon, Berks., 70 (n 355)
Peniston. *See* Penyston
Penny, Edward, curate of Islip, 25, 36, 64 (n 240)
Penyston, Sir Fairmedow, 13 (2), 54 (n 98)
Penyston, Sir Thomas, xxv, 54 (n 98)
Percey, John, of Caversham, 8

INDEX OF PERSONS

Percey, Robert, of Caversham, 8
Phillips, Thomas, of Caversham, 8
Poltin, William, of Heythrop, 29–30, 60 (n 194)
Potter, William, of Tadmarton, 44, 45, 71 (n 375)
Prentice, Anne, of Deddington, 55 (n 108)
Prentice, Anthony, of Deddington, 14, 55 (n 108)
Pufford, William, of Spelsbury, 29

Read, Elizabeth, of Enstone, 16
Read, William, of Enstone, 16
Redrobe, Edward, xxviii
Reeve, Joan, of Great Tew, xxvi
Reeve, Thomas, of Great Tew, xxiii (2), xxvi
Rews. *See* Rowse
Reynolds, Ann, of Cassington, 66 (n 268)
Reynolds, Christopher, of Cassington, 65 (n 268)
Reynolds, Edmund, of Cassington, 66 (n 268)
Reynolds, Thomas, vicar of Aston Rowant, xxxvi, xxxviii (2), 3, 5, 49 (n 12)
Reynolds family, of Cassington, 65 (n 268)
Richardson, John, of Watlington, 65 (n 255)
Righton, Mary, of Enstone, 16, 56 (n 122)
Righton, Robert, of Enstone, 16
Robbins, Joseph, of Burford, 61 (n 207)
Rochester, Earl and Countess of. *See* Wilmot
Roe, Sir Thomas, xxv
Rogers, Robert, nonconformist minister, 66 (n 270)
Round, John, of Harpsden, 57 (n 140)
Rowell, Margaret, 12, 54 (n 96)
Rowse, Elizabeth, of Deddington, 55 (n 108)
Rowse, John, of Deddington, 14, 55 (n 104)
Rowse, William, of Deddington, 14, 55 (ns 105–6, 108)
Rundle, Thomas, of Bloxham, 51 (n 49)
Ryton. *See* Righton

Salmon, Nathaniel, xi–xii
Salter, Nicholas, of Caversham, 9
Sancroft, William, Archbishop of Canterbury, xxvii, xxviii, xxix, xxxvii
Savadge, Anne, of Fringford, 56 (n 131)
Savadge, Robin, of Fringford, 18, 56 (n 131)
Saye and Sele, Lord. *See* Fiennes
Sayer, Peter, of Sandford on Thames, 39
Scott, Anne, of Spelsbury, 29
Scott, James, Duke of Monmouth, xxx, 49 (n 20)
Scrope, Col. Adrian, xx, 70 (n 346)
Scudder, Richard, of Charlbury, 10, 53 (n 76)
Seacole, Robert, of Shipton under Wychwood, 44, 71 (n 367)
Secker, Thomas, Archbishop of Canterbury, xl
  visitation (1738), 48–73 *passim*
Shaftesbury, Earl of. *See* Cooper
Sheldon, Edward, of Steeple Barton, 66 (n 281)
Sheldon, Gilbert, Archbishop of Canterbury, xii, xiv, xviii, xix
Sheldon, Ralph, of Steeple Barton, 66 (n 281)
Shelley, Peter, curate of Caversham, xxxii (2), 10, 52 (n 66), 58 (n 162)
Shepherd, Catherine, of South Leigh, 61 (n 210)

INDEX OF PERSONS

Shepherd, William, of South Leigh, 61 (n 210)
Shod, Elizabeth, of Charlbury, 53 (n 74)
Shod, Henry, of Charlbury, 10, 53 (n 74)
Sidwell, John, of Bampton, 5, 51 (n 40)
Simmons, Thomas, of Caversham, 9
Sims, John, of Kidlington, 66 (n 274)
Skinner, Robert, Bishop of Worcester, xxxv (n 127)
Skinner, William, of Bampton, 5, 51 (n 40)
Slater, Elizabeth, of Bladon, 65 (n 259)
Slater, Thomas, of Bladon, 65 (n 259)
Smalbone, Jonas, of Duns Tew, 15, 56 (n 118)
Smalbone, Sarah, of Duns Tew, 15, 56 (n 118)
Smith, Anne, of Hethe, 21
Smith, Edward, of Deddington, 14
Smith, John, rector of Woodeaton, 31, 60 (n 200)
Smith, Richard, of Stokenchurch, xxii (n 55), 65 (n 252)
Snadhams, Athanasius, of Caversham, 8
Snell, Thomas, vicar of Bampton, 50 (n 23)
Soundy, Richard, of Caversham, 8, 52 (n 61)
Stafford, William, of Aston Rowant, 4, 5
Stamp, —, of Abingdon, Berks., 43
Stannett. *See* Stennett
Statham, Samuel, of Banbury, 1, 48 (n 5)
Statsfield, Robin, of Fringford, 18, 56 (n 129)
Stedham. *See* Statham
Stennett, Edward, xxi, 7, 52 (n 52)
Stephens, John, of Caversham, 8
Stevens, Thomas, of Caversham, 9
Stevens, Thomas, of Lewknor, 40, 69 (n 342)
Stevens, William, of Caversham, 9
Strange, Francis, of Charlbury, 10, 53 (n 75)
Stranke, Thomas, of Milcombe, 51 (n 42)
Stratford, William, xiii
Strength. *See* Strange
Sturch, John, of Wigginton, 63 (n 222)
Sutton, James, of Banbury, xxi (n 52), 55 (n 114)
Swift, Joyce, of Adderbury, 44, 71 (n 370)
Swinnock, George, nonconformist minister, xvi–xvii, xviii, 41, 47

Taylor, Alice, of Spelsbury, 29
Taylor, Nicholas, of Spelsbury, 29, 60 (n 193)
Taylor, Thomas, of North Leigh, 46, 72 (n 401)
Thackham, Thomas, vicar of Broadwell, 33, 35, 61 (n 204)
Thomas, William, of Minster Lovell, 66 (n 275)
Thomlinson, Thomas, rector of South Weston, xxxix, 31, 60 (n 199)
Thorley, John, of Chipping Norton, 62 (n 215), 70 (n 360)
Thorp, John, vicar of Burford, 33, 61 (n 205)
Tidmarsh, Giles, of Chipping Norton, xxiii, 62 (n 215)
Tidmarsh, Susanna, of Sarsden, 29, 60 (n 188)
Tidmarsh, William, of Sarsden, 29
Titmarsh, Richard, of Oxford (St Thomas), 68 (n 322)
Tomkins, John, of Abingdon, Berks., 43, 70 (n 354)
Toms, Thomas, of Deddington, 14
Triplet, Thomas, of Deddington, 14

Troughton, John, nonconformist minister, xv, xvi, xviii (2), 47 (2), 71 (n 385)
True, John, of Bampton, 50 (n 29)
True, Ruth, of Bampton, 5, 50 (n 29)
Tucker, Francis, of Swyncombe, 35, 36 (2)
Turner, John, of Black Bourton, 5, 51 (n 42)
Turner, Lucy, of Black Bourton, 51 (n 42)
Turner, Thomas, Archdeacon of Essex, xxxi (n 106)
Turner, Walter, of Black Bourton, 51 (n 42)
Turner, William, of Aston Rowant, 4, 35, 36, 49 (ns 14, 22), 64 (n 232)
Tustle, James, of Charlbury, 10
Tyler, John, of Henley, 63 (n 231)
Tyrer, Edward, vicar of Clanfield, xxxiii, xxxvi, 12, 54 (n 91)

Venner, Thomas, xxiv, xxv, xl
Verney, Edmund, of Claydon, Bucks., xxvi
Vernon, George, rector of Sarsden, xxxix (3), xl, 29, 60 (n 191)
Vicaris, Robert, rector of Heythrop, xxxvi, 30, 60 (n 195)

Waller. *See* Walter
Walter, Sir William, 29, 60 (n 189)
Walters, William, of Henley, 40, 69 (n 329)
Wansel, Richard, of Sarsden, 29
Wansel, Susanna, of Sarsden, 29, 60 (n 188)
Ward, Benjamin, 45, 71 (ns 376-77)
Ward, John, of Hethe, 21
Ward, Seth, Bishop of Salisbury, xxix
Warner, William, of South Newington, 68 (n 311)
Warwick, William, of Bampton, xxiv, 5, 50 (n 33)
Watts, Ann, of Bampton, 5, 50 (n 28)
Watts, Elizabeth, of Bampton, 50 (n 28)
Wellicom, Margaret, of Bampton, 5, 51 (n 37)
Wellicom, William, of Bampton, 5, 51 (n 37)
Wells, Samuel, nonconformist minister, xv, xviii (2), xxi (n 52), xxiii, 45, 47, 55 (ns 111, 114), 56 (n 127)
West, Gregory, of Watlington, 40, 69 (n 340)
Westbury, George, of Wigginton, 63 (n 222)
Weston, Elizabeth, 12, 54 (n 96)
Weston, George, of Combe, xxii (n 56), xxiii, 12, 54 (ns 95-96)
Weston, James, 12
Weston, Robert, 12, 54 (ns 95-96)
Weston, William, of Banbury, xxi (n 52)
Wharton, Philip, 4th Baron Wharton, xvi (n 25), xvii
Whately, Samuel, of Deddington, 14, 34, 55 (n 109)
Whately, Thomas, nonconformist minister, xxxiv, xxxvi, 1, 12, 34, 45, 46, 47 (2), 48 (n 4), 55 (n 111)
Whately, William, vicar of Banbury, 48 (n 4)
Wheate, Jeremiah, vicar of Deddington, xxxii, xxxvii, 14, 55 (n 110)
Wheately. *See* Whately
Wheeler, Henry, of Bampton, 5, 50 (n 26)
Wheeler, John, of Alvescot, xxiv, 50 (n 25)
Wheeler, Samuel, of Burford, 61 (n 207)
White, Anne, of Charlbury 10, 53 (n 80)
Wicks, Thomas, of Caversham, 9
Wilcocks, Joseph, Bishop of Gloucester, xiii

INDEX OF PERSONS

William III, 49 (n 20)
Williams, —, of Bampton, 5
Williams, Hannah, of Cote, 50 (n 24)
Williams, Roger, of Minster Lovell, 66 (n 275)
Williamson, Sir Joseph, 72 (n 393)
Willicome. *See* Wellicom
Willier, William, of Caversham, 9
Willmore. *See* Wilmot
Wilmot, Anne, Countess of Rochester, 48 (n 6)
Wilmot, Benjamin, of Hook Norton, 70 (n 363)
Wilmot, James, of Hook Norton, 44, 45, 70 (n 363), 71 (n 380)
Wilmot, John, 2nd Earl of Rochester, 48 (n 6)
Wilmot, Samuel, of Hook Norton, 45, 70 (n 364), 71 (n 380)
Window, Elizabeth, of Bampton, 5, 50 (n 27)
Window, Richard, of Bampton, 5, 50 (n 27)
Wing, Charles, of Witney, 61 (n 211)
Winter, Francis, of Deddington, 14
Winterbourne, Bridget, of Weald, 51 (n 41)
Winterbourne, Robert, of Weald, 5, 51 (n 41)
Wise, Edward, of Cogges, 47, 73 (n 405)
Wise, Joseph, of Berrick Salome, 7, 52 (n 51)
Wise, William, of Bampton, xxiv, 5, 50 (n 31)
Wood, Anthony, xii (n 6), xiii (n 11), xv, xvi
Worden, Thomas, nonconformist minister, 43, 70 (n 361)
Wren, Sir Christopher, xiii
Wyer, Mrs, of Deddington, 46, 72 (n 396)

INDEX OF PLACES

(All places in Oxfordshire, before 1974, unless otherwise stated)

Abingdon, Berks., xvi, xvii, xxix (3), 43 (3), 47, 70 (n 346)
Adderbury, xiv, xv (2), xix, xx (2), xxi, xxxiii, xxxiv (2), xxxvii, xxxviii (3), xl, 1–2, 34, 35, 44–45, 48 (ns 1, 6, 7), 51 (ns 46–47), 52 (n 49), 59 (n 183), 71 (n 370)
Adwell, 37, 60 (n 198), 71 (n 373)
Alvescot, xxiv, xxvi, 37, 50 (ns 25, 28, 30, 31), 51 (n 45), 61 (n 208), 65 (n 258)
Ambrosden, xvii, 63 (n 229)
Asthall, 37, 65 (n 257)
Aston (in Bampton parish), 5, 50 (n 24), 51 (ns 36, 39)
Aston deanery, xxxiii, 35, 36, 37, 60 (n 197)
Aston Rowant, xiv, xxvi, xxix, xxxiv (2), xxxvi, xxxviii (2), xl, xli (n 164), 2–5, 35, 36, 37, 49 (ns 12, 22)
Aylesbury, Bucks., xvii

Bampton, xxiii, xxvi, xxxvi (n 139), xl, 5, 37, 50 (ns 24–25), 65 (n 258)
Banbury, xv (2), xviii, xix (and n 44), xxi, xxiii, xxiv, xxv, xxxiii (n 120), xxxvii (2), xl, xli, 1, 14, 18, 48 (ns 4–5), 55 (ns 111, 114), 56 (n 127), 68 (n 312), 71 (ns 375–76)
Barford St John, 39
Barford St Michael, 39, 55 (n 110)
Beckley, xxvii
Begbroke, 37, 65 (n 260)
Berkshire, 70 (n 361)
Berrick Salome, 7, 37, 52 (ns 50–51)
Bicester, xiv, xv, xvi, xvii, xviii, xx, xxi, xxxiii, xl, 21, 26, 46–47, 71 (n 385), 72 (n 393)
Bicester deanery, xxxiii, 34, 36, 38
Bix, 37, 64 (n 246)
Black Bourton, xxvii (n 90), xxxix (n 158), 5–6, 37, 51 (n 45)
Bladon, xxix, xli, 37, 65 (n 259)
Bledlow, Bucks., xvii
Bletchingdon, 38, 53 (n 70)
Bloxham, xiv, xviii, xx (2), xxvi, xxxv (n 126), xxxvi (and n 139), xl, 6–7, 39, 44–45, 51 (ns 48–49), 71 (n 373)
Bodicote, 48 (n 7)
Bourton on the Water, Gloucs., xxxix, 60 (n 191), 70 (n 358)
Brackley, Northants., xvii
Brighthampton, 50 (n 24)
Brize Norton, xiv, xxiv, xxvii (n 90), 37, 46–47, 61 (n 207), 65 (n 262), 72 (n 399)
Broadwell, 37, 61 (n 204), 65 (n 261)
Broughton Poggs, 37, 71 (n 375)
Buckinghamshire, 40
Burdrop, 44–45
Burford, xxii (n 56), xxiv (2), xxxiv (3), xl, 33, 35, 37, 57 (n 135), 61 (ns 205, 207–8), 65 (n 258)
Burton Dassett, Warws., xvii

INDEX OF PLACES 87

Calthorpe House, Banbury, xxxvii, 18, 56 (n 134)
Cambridge University
  Pembroke College, 53 (n 70)
  Sidney College, 55 (n 110)
Cassington, xxvii (n 90), 38, 65 (n 268)
Caversfield, xv
Caversham, xix, xxvi, xxvii (n 90), xxxii, xli, 7–10, 52 (ns 62, 65), 53 (n 67)
Chadlington, xviii, xx (2), 11, 39, 42–43, 53 (n 71), 60 (n 188)
Chalgrove, xxvii (n 90), xxxvi, xli, 7, 52 (n 50)
Charlbury, xiv, xviii, xx, xxi, xxii (n 55), xxxiv (2), xl, 10–11, 33, 35, 39, 42–43, 53 (ns 71–72), 56 (n 126), 62 (n 215)
Chastleton, xxxiii, 11, 54 (n 85)
Chilson, 10
Chimney, 50 (n 24)
Chinnor, xxii, 11, 37, 54 (ns 87, 89)
Chipping Norton, xiv, xv, xviii, xxi (2), xxiii, xxiv (2), xxviii, xxxiii, xxxiv (2), xl, 10, 34, 42–43, 59 (n 186), 60 (ns 188, 195), 62 (n 215), 70 (n 360)
Chipping Norton deanery, xxxiii, 34
Clanfield, xxiv, xxxiii, xxxvi, 5, 11–12, 38, 51 (n 43), 54 (n 92)
Clifton, 55 (ns 108, 111)
Cogges, xiv, xv (3), xvi (3), xviii, xx, xxiv, 46–47, 70 (n 358), 72 (n 403), 73 (ns 404–6)
Combe, xxii (n 56), 12–13, 38, 48 (n 4), 54 (ns 93–94)
Compton, Berks., 59 (n 180)
Cornwell, xxxiii, 13, 39, 54 (n 98), 55 (n 100)
Cote, 50 (n 24), 61 (n 209)
Cottisford, 34, 36, 38, 67 (n 295)
Cowley, xxiii, xxvii (n 90)
Cuddesdon, xiv
Cuddesdon deanery, xxxiii
Cuddington. *See* Kiddington
Cuxham, 49 (n 21), 64 (n 244)

Deddington, xiv, xv, xx, xxi, xxiii, xxxii, xxxvi, xxxvii, xl, 13–14, 46–47, 55 (ns 105, 110–11), 56 (n 122), 72 (n 396)
Deddington deanery, xxxiii, 34, 35
Devizes, Wilts., xxix
Dorchester, xix (n 44), xxi, xxxiii (n 120), 52 (n 53), 70 (n 349)
Drayton, xxxvii (2), 14–15, 51 (n 42), 55 (n 115), 56 (n 116), 71 (n 377)
Ducklington, 38, 66 (n 269)
Duns Tew, xxxvi, 15, 38, 56 (n 117)

Elton, Herefs., 69 (n 331)
Ely, Cambs., 53 (n 70)
Enstone, xxxvi, xxxvii, xxxix, 16–17, 34, 56 (ns 121, 126)
Epwell, xxxv (n 126), 34, 35, 39, 62 (n 221)
Eton College, Bucks., 64 (n 237)
Ewelme, 63 (n 231)

Faringdon, Berks., 70 (n 355)
Fawler, 11
Filkins, 6, 51 (n 43), 59 (n 166)
Finedon, Northants., 52 (n 66)
Finstock, xxi, 11, 54 (n 83)

INDEX OF PLACES

Forest Hill, 60 (n 199)
Fringford, xxxvi, 17–18, 38, 56 (ns 127–28)

Gagingwell, 51 (n 42)
Gloucester
  Dean and Chapter, xxviii (2)
  Parishes of St John and St Michael, xxxix, 60 (n 191)
Gloucestershire, 39, 70 (n 361)
Godington, 38, 57 (n 141), 67 (n 288)
Great Rissington, Gloucs., 61 (n 207)
Great Rollright, xxviii, 62 (n 217)
Great Tew, xxiii, xxxv (n 126), 34, 35, 39, 63 (n 223), 68 (n 312)
Grendon Underwood, Bucks., xvii

Hampton Gay, 38
Hampton Poyle, 38, 58 (n 165), 67 (n 289)
Hanborough, 38, 66 (n 270)
Hanwell, xxxii, xxxvi, xxxvii, xli, 18–20, 57 (ns 136–37)
Hardwick, 34, 36, 57 (n 141), 63 (ns 226–28)
Harpsden, xxxvii, 20–21, 57 (ns 139–40)
Hazleton, Gloucs., 70 (n 358)
Headington, 39, 68 (n 314)
Heath. *See* Hethe
Hempton, 1, 46–47, 48 (n 4), 55 (ns 107, 111)
Henley deanery, xxxiii, 34–35, 36, 37
Henley on Thames, xiv (2), xv, xviii, xx (2), xxi (2), xxxiii, xxxiv (2), xl, xli, 7, 34, 36, 37, 40–41, 63 (n 231), 70 (n 346)
Hethe, xxxi, xxxvii, xxxviii (2), 21–22, 38, 59 (n 167)
Heyford, xxxiv (2), xli (n 164), 34, 36, 63 (n 225), 72 (n 390)
Heythrop, 29, 60 (ns 195–96)
High Wycombe, Bucks., xvii (2)
Hockley, Essex, xxxi (n 106)
Hook Norton, xiv (2), xx, xxviii, xxxv (n 126), xl, xli, 34, 38, 44, 45 (2), 57 (n 135), 62 (n 217), 70 (n 363), 71 (ns 376, 379)

Ibstone, Bucks., xxxii, xxxviii (2), xli, 22–24, 58 (ns 153, 163)
Islip, xxxiii, 24–25, 34, 36, 58 (n 164)

Jevington, Sussex, 56 (n 119)

Kencot, 25, 58 (n 166)
Kiddington, 33, 35, 38, 62 (n 212)
Kidlington, 38
Kidmore End, 52 (n 57)
Kingham, 39, 67 (n 305)
Kingston Blount, xx, 3 (2), 42–43, 49 (n 11)
Kirtlington, 38, 67 (n 285)

Launton, 38, 67 (n 286)
Leafield, xl, 10, 53 (n 68)
Leicester, Leics., 48 (n 5)
Lew, 50 (ns 24, 31), 51 (n 34)
Lewknor, xiv, xviii, xx, xxvi, xxxix, xl, 25–26, 37, 40–41, 58 (n 153), 59 (n 169)
Lillingstone Lovell, 38, 64 (n 239), 67 (n 291)

Lincoln,
  Bishop of, 69 (n 333)
  Dean and Chapter of, 69 (n 333)
Little Shelford, Cambs., 52 (n 55)
London, xvii, xxiii, xxiv, 18, 40, 56 (n 124), 57 (n 141), 62 (n 215), 69 (n 331)
  St Giles, Cripplegate, 48 (n 5)
Longworth, Berks., 70 (n 355)
Loughborough, Leics., 48 (n 5)
Lower Heyford. *See* Heyford
Lower Swell, Gloucs., xxix

Malmesbury, Wilts., 73 (n 411)
Mapledurham, 52 (n 57)
Middleton Stoney, xxxi, xxxiii, 26–27, 59 (n 179)
Milcombe, xxxv (n 126), 39, 51 (ns 42, 49)
Milton (in Adderbury parish), 48 (ns 3, 7)
Milton under Wychwood, xxiv, 44, 53 (ns 68, 71–72), 65 (n 258), 71 (n 367), 72 (n 399)
Minster Lovell, 38, 66 (n 275)
Mixbury, 38, 67 (n 292)
Mongewell, xxxiii, 27, 59 (n 181)
Moreton in Marsh, Gloucs., 70 (n 363)

Nazeing, Essex, xxxii (n 113)
Nether Worton, 32
Nettlebed, 64 (n 231)
Newbury, Berks., xxix, 52 (n 52)
North Aston, 33, 35, 62 (n 213), 64 (n 235)
North Leigh, xiv, 46–47, 72 (n 400)
North Stoke, 37, 64 (n 250)
Northamptonshire, xxxvii
Nuffield, 61 (n 204)
Nuneham Courtenay, 39

Oddington, Gloucs., 48 (n 6)
Over Worton, 32, 60 (n 202)
Oxford City, xv, xvi, xxi, xxiii, xxiv, xxx (2), xxxiii (2), xli, 35, 60 (n 200), 70 (n 348)
  gaol, xxiii, xxiv (2), xxvi, 54 (n 95), 61 (n 208), 62 (n 215), 72 (n 399)
  parishes:
    Holywell, 39, 68 (n 318)
    St Clement, xxvii, 39, 68 (n 318)
    St Ebbe, 39, 68 (n 321)
    St Giles, 39, 69 (n 324)
    St Martin, 39, 69 (n 325)
    St Mary Magdalen, xxvii (n 90), 39, 68 (n 323)
    St Michael, xxii (n 55), 39, 68 (n 319)
    St Peter in the East, 39, 68 (n 320)
    St Thomas, 39
  Thame Street, xvi, xviii
Oxford deanery, xxxiii
Oxford University, xi–xii, xv, xvi, xviii
  colleges:
    All Souls', 50 (n 23), 59 (n 177)
    Balliol, 59 (ns 168, 184), 60 (n 200)
    Brasenose, 58 (n 162)

INDEX OF PLACES

    Christ Church, xi (4), xii (3), xiii, xvi (2), xvii, xxvii, xxix, 51 (n 44), 52 (n 66), 54 (n 99), 59 (n 178)
    Corpus Christi, 51 (n 48), 54 (n 93), 58 (n 165), 72 (n 390)
    Exeter, 50 (n 23)
    Jesus, 57 (n 180)
    Lincoln, 57 (n 139)
    Magdalen, 56 (n 126), 58 (n 150), 60 (n 200), 64 (n 235)
    Pembroke, xvi, 49 (n 12), 59 (n 187)
    Queen's, 60 (n 199)
    St John's, xv
    University, 54 (n 84)
    Wadham, 56 (n 119), 57 (n 136), 61 (n 203)
  halls:
    Magdalen, 52 (n 55), 71 (n 373), 73 (n 411)
    New Inn, 48 (n 4)
Oxford University Press, xii

Passenham, Northants., xvii
Peterborough diocese, xix
Piddington, 34, 36, 63 (ns 229–30)
Priors Marston, Warws., xvii
Pyrton, xxvii, 37, 64 (n 251)

Radford, 16
Reading, Berks., xxix, 70 (ns 346, 355)
Rousham, 27–28, 38, 59 (n 185)

Salford, xxxiii, 28–29, 39, 59 (n 186), 64 (n 242)
Sampford Peverell, Devon, 52 (n 53)
Sandford on Thames, 39, 68 (n 315)
Sandford St Martin, 38, 63 (n 223)
Sarsden, xxxix, 29, 60 (n 192)
Shabbington, Bucks., 48 (n. 6)
Shifford, 50 (n 24)
Shilton, 50 (n 24)
Shipton under Wychwood, xiv, xx, 39, 44–45, 53 (n 68)
Shorthampton, 11
Shutford, 62 (n 221), 71 (n 374)
Sibford Ferris, 62 (n 221)
Sibford Gower, xiv, xviii, xx, 34, 35, 44–45, 62 (n 221), 71 (n 381), 72 (n 401)
Somerton, 38, 57 (n 141), 67 (n 293)
Sondcomb. *See* Swyncombe
Souldern, 38, 67 (n 294)
South Leigh, 33, 35, 38, 61 (n 210)
South Newington, xxxv (n 126), 39, 68 (n 311), 71 (n 377)
South Stoke, xxvii (n 90)
South Weston, 30–31, 37, 60 (n 197)
Southsea, Hants., xvii
Spelsbury, xxvii (n 90), xxxvi, 29–30, 60 (ns 195–96)
Standlake, 33, 35, 38, 61 (n 209)
Stanton Harcourt, xxiii, 38, 61 (n 211), 66 (n 277)
Stanton St John, 39
Steeple Aston, 38, 64 (n 242), 67 (ns 296–97)
Steeple Barton, 38, 66 (n 281)

Stoke Lyne, 38
Stokenchurch, xxii (n 56), xxix, 22, 37, 65 (n 252)
Stonesfield, 12–13, 38, 54 (ns 93–94)
Stow on the Wold, Gloucs., xxix (2)
Suadecliffe. *See* Swalcliffe
Sulgrave, Northants., xvii
Sutton under Brailes, Warws., 48 (n 4)
Swalcliffe, xiv, xx, 34, 35, 39, 44–45, 62 (n 221)
Swerford, 39, 67 (n 309)
Swyncombe, 35, 36, 37, 65 (n 253)

Tadmarton, xiv (2), xx, 44–45, 71 (n 374)
Taynton, 38, 66 (n 283)
Thame, xiv, xv, xvii (2), xviii, xix (n 44), xx, xxi, xxvi, xxxiii (n 120), xli, 40–41, 69 (n 333)
Towcester, Northants., xvii
Tubney, Berks., xvi
Tur Langton, Leics., 67 (n 300)

Upper Winchendon, Bucks., xvi (n 25)

Waddesdon, Bucks., xvii, 48 (n 6)
Wallingford, Berks., xxi, 7, 52 (n 52)
Wanlip, Leics., xvii
Warborough, xiv (2), xv, xviii, xx (3), xxi, xxiii, xl, 7, 42–43, 70 (n 349)
Warminster, Wilts., xxix
Warwickshire, 57 (n 135), 66 (n 281), 70 (n 361)
Waterperry, 39, 69 (n 327)
Watlington, xiv, xv, xviii, xx, xxi (3), xxii, 37, 40–41, 52 (ns 52–53), 64 (n 242), 65 (n 255)
Weald, xxiv, 50 (n 25), 51 (n 41)
Westbury, Bucks., xvii
Westwell, xxvii (n 90)
Whitwell, Derby., 57 (n 139)
Wigginton, xxxv (n 126), 34, 35, 39, 63 (n 222)
Wilcote, xiv, xv, xx, 46–47
Winterborne Monkton, Wilts., 61 (n 211)
Witney, xx, xxvi (2), xxxiii, xxxiv (2), xl, xli, 25, 27, 33, 35 (2), 54 (n 93), 61 (ns 208, 211), 65 (n 258), 68 (n 312), 72 (n 403), 73 (ns 404, 406, 411)
Witney deanery, xxxiii, 33, 35, 37–38
Wolvercote, 39, 69 (n 326)
Woodeaton, xxxiii, 31, 60 (ns 200–1)
Woodford, Essex, 52 (n 66)
Woodstock, xxix, xli, 38, 66 (n 284)
Woodstock deanery, xxxiii, 33, 35
Wormsley House, Lewknor, xx, 40–41, 70 (n 346)
Worton, 32
Wroxton, xvii (n 90)

INDEX OF SUBJECTS

Allegiance, oath of, xxiii (2), 70 (n 350)
Anabaptists, xx, xxix, xxxi (n 106), xxxii, xxxvi (2), xxxvii, xxxviii, xl, 3–5, 6, 14 (3), 15, 18, 19, 25 (2), 26, 29, 32, 33, 35, 39, 40 (3), 42 (2), 44 (4), 46, 49 (n 22), 50 (n 24), 51 (n 49), 53 (n 67), 55 (n 111), 56 (ns 130, 135), 57 (n 137), 59 (ns 169, 173), 61 (ns 207, 209, 211), 62 (ns 217, 221), 65 (ns 252, 255, 257–58, 262), 66 (ns 268–70), 68 (ns 311, 314, 322), 70 (n 358), 71 (n 379), 72 (n 403), 73 (n 406). *See also* Baptists
Atheists, 26, 51 (n 40)

Baptists, xx, xxi (4), xxiv–xxv, 51 (n 49), 52 (n 52), 54 (ns 83, 89), 69 (n 326), 70 (ns 346, 354–55, 360, 363), 71 (n 379). *See also* Anabaptists

Church rates, xxiii, 37, 66 (n 283), 72 (n 401)
Churchwardens, xxii (2), xxiv, xxx (2), xxxiv (2), xxxviii (2), xxxix, 2–3, 4, 9, 15, 16, 21, 26, 34, 36 (2), 38, 39, 49 (n 8), 52 (n 53), 54 (n 86), 59 (n 187), 60 (ns 195, 198), 64 (ns 242, 246, 250), 65 (n 253), 67 (ns 297, 305), 68 (ns 317–19, 321, 323), 69 (ns 324, 326)
Compton Census (1676), ix, xix, 48–73 *passim*
Congregationalists. *See* Independents
Constables, parish, xxiv, xxvi, xxxix, 4, 8, 52 (n 60), 53 (n 72)
Conventicle Acts, (1664), xxii
   (1670), xxii, xxiii, xxiv, xxxvii

Excommunication, excommunicated persons, xxii, xxxv, 15, 18, 19, 35, 38 (3), 50 (ns 27, 30), 51 (ns 35, 49), 53 (ns 68, 71–72, 74–75, 77, 80–81), 54 (ns 82, 86, 95), 56 (ns 117–18, 128–31), 57 (ns 137, 140, 143, 146), 58 (n 164), 60 (n 193), 61 (ns 206–9), 62 (ns 215, 217), 63 (ns 222, 225), 64 (ns 231, 233, 251), 65 (ns 252, 255), 66 (ns 268, 275, 279, 281), 67 (ns 286, 288, 293, 300), 68 (ns 311–12, 319, 322–23), 69 (ns 325, 329, 338–40), 70 (ns 353, 357, 363–64), 71 (ns 365, 376–77, 383–85), 72 (ns 386, 399, 401), 73 (n 405)

Five Mile Act (1665), xv, xxii, xxiii

Heathens, 5

Independents, Congregationalists, xv, xvi (n 25), xx, xxi (5), xl, xli, 7, 10 (2), 32, 42 (2), 46, 52 (n 53), 61 (n 207), 62 (ns 211, 215), 63 (n 231), 65 (n 255), 67 (n 284), 69 (n 333), 70 (ns 360–61)
Indulgence, declaration of, xxi, xxiii, xxiv, 32, 48 (n 5), 68 (n 323)

Justices of the Peace, magistrates, xxiii, xxiv, xxv (3), xxvi, xxxvii (2), xxxix (2), 2, 4, 11, 18, 23, 26, 40

Papists, popish recusants. *See* Roman Catholics
Presbyterians, xv, xvi, xxi (2), xxxii, xxxvii, xl, xli, 1–2, 14, 40 (3), 42 (2), 44, 46 (2), 48 (n 3), 51 (n 49), 53 (ns 67, 71), 55 (ns 111, 114), 56 (ns 135), 57 (n 140), 61 (ns 207, 211),

INDEX OF SUBJECTS 93

62 (n 215), 63 (n 231), 65 (ns 255, 262), 66 (ns 277, 279, 284), 67 (n 300), 68 (n 311), 72 (ns 385, 395), 73 (n 411)

Quakers, xv, xix, xxi (2), xxii (2), xxiii (2), xxiv, xxv, xxvi (4), xxix, xxxiii, xxxiv, xxxvi, xxxvii (2), xxxviii (2), xxxix (n 158), xl, 1, 5 (2), 6 (3), 7, 8, 10 (2), 11, 12 (2), 14 (3), 18, 19, 25, 27, 30–31, 32 (2), 35, 37 (5), 38 (4), 39 (3), 40, 42 (3), 44 (5), 46 (2), 48 (ns 1–2), 50 (ns 24–25, 31, 33), 51 (ns 42–43, 45, 49), 52 (ns 50, 61), 53 (ns 67–68, 71–73), 54 (ns 89, 96), 55 (ns 108, 111, 114), 56 (n 122), 59 (ns 166, 183, 185), 60 (ns 189, 197–98), 61 (ns 207–8, 211), 62 (ns 215, 217, 221), 63 (ns 225, 231), 64 (ns 244, 246), 65 (ns 252, 258, 261), 66 (ns 269, 274, 279, 281, 283), 67 (n 291), 68 (n 309, 311–12, 314, 318, 323), 69 (ns 324, 333), 70 (n 350), 71 (ns 365, 367, 370, 374–77, 381, 385), 72 (ns 399–401, 403)

Quarter Sessions, xxiii, xxvi (2), xxxix, 50 (n 30), 51 (ns 35, 41–43)

Roman Catholics, xiv, xix (2), xxi, xxii, xxvi, xxxii, xxxiv, xxxvi, xxxviii, xl, 5, 7, 8, 10, 12, 13, 21, 23, 33 (2), 37, 38 (3), 39, 48 (n 7), 50 (n 24), 52 (ns 50, 57), 53 (n 67), 54 (ns 88, 94, 97), 55 (n 111), 56 (n 128), 57 (ns 141–43, 145), 58 (ns 151, 154, 163–64), 59 (n 181), 62 (ns 212–13), 63 (n 226), 64 (n 251), 65 (ns 253, 257, 261–62, 268), 66 (ns 267–70, 279, 281, 284), 67 (ns 285–86, 288, 293–95), 68 (ns 312, 315–22)

Sabbatarians, xx, xxi, 7, 23, 25, 40, 42 (2), 52 (ns 50–51), 58 (n 154), 65 (n 255)

Tithes, xxiii, 24, 53 (n 72), 58 (ns 157, 159–61), 71 (n 375), 72 (n 401)

Visitations, archidiaconal, xxxiv (2), xxxviii, 35–39, 49 (n 8)
    episcopal, xxx, xxxi, xxxiii, xxxiv (2), xxxv, xxxviii, 33–35, 49 (n 8), 63 (n 224)